Jewelry Weaving for Everyone

Techniques and Patterns

Rita Scher

ACKNOWLEDGEMENTS

This book could not have been accomplished without the assistance, support and encouragement of teachers, students, photographers and friends.

To my family, I wish to thank them all, especially Valerie, Harris, Evan, Aaron and Joshua.

Second Edition – 2006

Published by Jay Street Publishers
155 West 72nd Street, New York, NY 10023

ISBN 1-889534-91-9

On First Page: Gold Filigree Necklace

Reviews

"Let the fun begin! This exciting book allows even the beginner to create beautiful jewelry using a few simple tools that are lightweight and portable. Clear instructions and illustrations guide you step by step through each project. Get together with a group, have a cup of coffee and make a variety of necklaces, bracelets and earrings – using Rita's book!"

Elaine Kris Ludman
Enamelist
New York

"As a jeweler, fellow artist and Graduate Gemologist, over the years I have seen the beading industry explode into new territory of development and innovation in jewelry design. Rita Scher's book is an informative asset to this growing market and the need for the demonstration and development involved with wire weaving techniques and design. This book will remain an important part of my reference library on design, crafting and jewelry technique."

Kerry Bourgeois
Jewelry Designer/Metalsmith
Los Angeles, CA

"Weaving with wire is addictive – I am inspired to try all sorts of variations. I always carry the spool and wire with me and create while in a doctor's waiting room, on public transportation – anywhere! The process draws inquisitve and interested onlookers. I just love the technique and the finished products have all been very well received."

Lillian Cozzarelli
Jewelry Designer/Metalsmith
New York

"I was browsing through the Amazon web site looking for craft books. After reading the description for Rita Scher's book, I decided to buy it. It has been a delight! I have produced many beautiful pieces of jewelry and have gotten great compliments from friends. I found the instructions very clear and the book unique.

Margaret M. Coakley
Psychotherapist
New Harbor, Maine

"The innovative designs in this book are useful additions to any jewelers repertoire. Many of my students and I have made beautiful necklaces to enhance enameled jewelry."

Sandra Kravitz
Teacher and President of the Enamel Guild
North East USA

BOOK REVIEW

by Patricia White

If you're like me, your hands are always busy, even while relaxing. I think that's why crocheting became so popular; it was compact, repetitive, and required one tool. A go anywhere craft. When I was a kid, I carried my little red wooden spool and a ball of crochet thread on endless car trips to ease the boredom of a long ride. Unfortunately, the only design that grew out of my spool were yards of chained thread and hot plates. Move forward 40 years and the little red spool hasn't changed much, but the design possibilities are endless, thanks to Rita Scher.

In her new book, ***Jewelry Weaving for Everyone***, Rita describes the basic elements of weaving and crocheting on wooden spools, using beads and pearls, with silver, gold or even craft wire, to produce lovely necklaces, bracelets and earrings. This comprehensive book, written with simple easy-to-follow instructions, covers in detail over 55 different patterns. Each page has a photo of the necklaces, along with the directions and close-up of the spool with the wire looped into the pattern. Rita takes you through the removal from the spool, finishing and use of findings. The book closes with a complete list of supply sources and a beautiful close-up of the author. I guarantee there will be a spool in your pocket after buying this book.

In loving memory of my Mother and Father.

I dedicate this book to Myra and Jim.

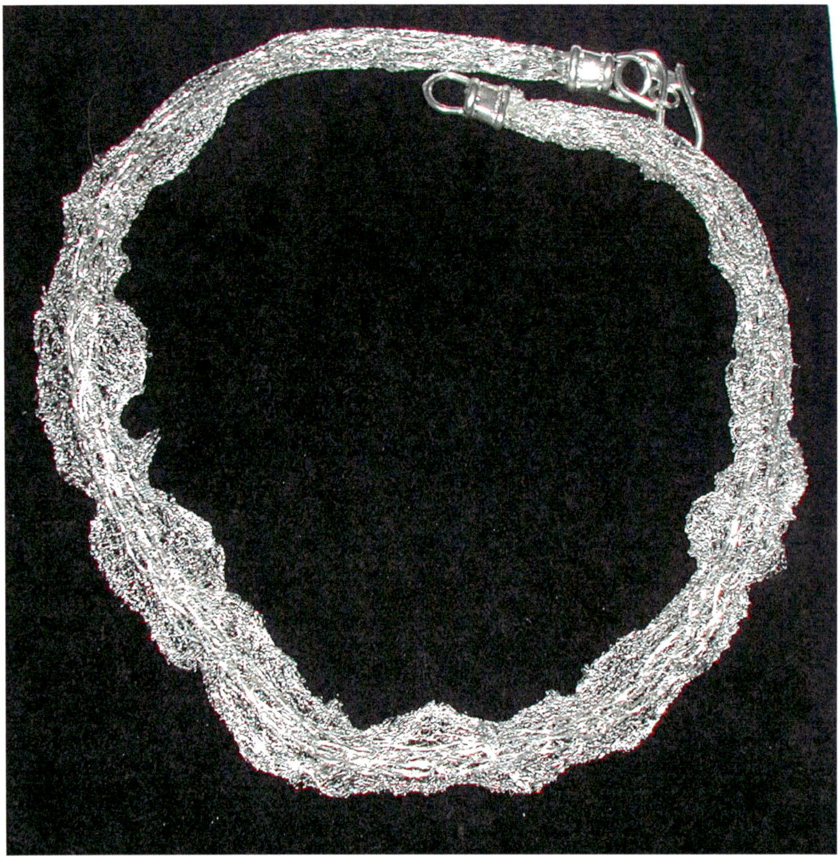

Mesh Necklace

TABLE OF CONTENTS

Pearl and Fine Silver; Triple Weave-in-Weave with East/West Pattern in Outside Weave

INTRODUCTION

This book describes the basic elements for wire weaving and crocheting with different size wooden spools, and will teach you the techniques and patterns to produce magnificent small and large necklaces, bracelets and earrings.

Using fine silver, gold, brass, copper, mesh and craft wire you will learn how to incorporate fresh water pearls, crystals, glass beads, and semi-precious stones into your work.

I. MATERIALS AND TOOLS

1. The following instructions will guide you on starting and completing your work, and the steps to take for the best results.

There are three kind of wooden spools *(Figure 1):* 3-prong, 4-prong and 5-prong spools. The 3-prong spool makes the smallest round design, the 4-prong a square design and the 5-prong a larger round design.

The prongs are made with cotter pins drilled into wooden spools. The wooden spools are made from local trees, never an endangered species.

The spools are then hand-polished using natural linseed oil. The results are a long lasting finish that is non-toxic and environmentally friendly. The spools are made in a seven-sided shape, which is easier to hold than the usual round shape made in the past.

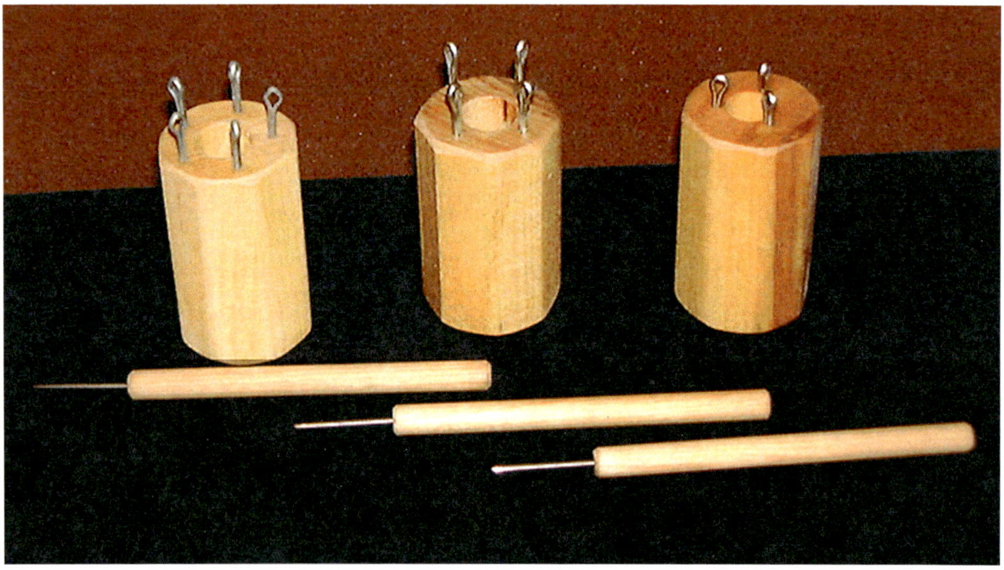

Figure 1. Spools (l to r): 5-Prong, 4-Prong, 3-Prong

Note: Wooden spools are available from Good Wood Looms in Langley, WA.
See Supply Source section.

2. Metal or craft wire: *(Figure 2)*

a. Fine silver 30-gauge for most patterns

b. Fine silver 24- or 26-gauge for weaving

c. Copper wire 30-gauge

d. 18K gold 30-gauge for most patterns 18K gold 24- or 26-gauge for weaving. You can also use 30-gauge gold-filled wire. (Optional)

e. Craft Black wire or any color (30-gauge or 32-gauge) available in most craft stores and usually made from copper wire, which is plastic coated. (Use Craft Black 26- or 28-gauge for practice.) Regarding 30-gauge brass wire, only use this for practice since over time it tarnishes.

3. Findings:
A variety of jump rings, endcaps and other findings: spring rings, lobster claws, heart shaped clasps etc. *(Figure 2)*

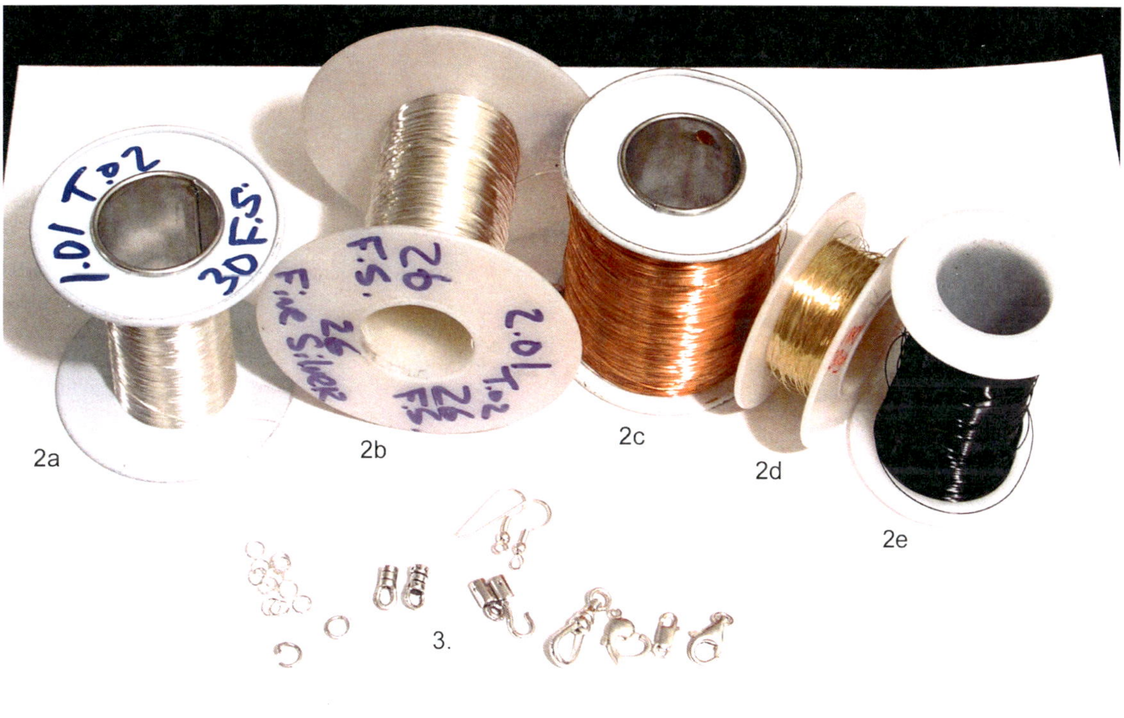

Figure 2

4. *(Figure 3)*

a. Pliers: Needle Nose (pointy), flat grooved that has a serrated edge.
b. Scissors (small), metal shears (very sharp).
c. Fine Tweezers
d. Cross Locking Tweezers
e. Solder Pick
f. Wooden Draw Plate
g. Measuring Tape

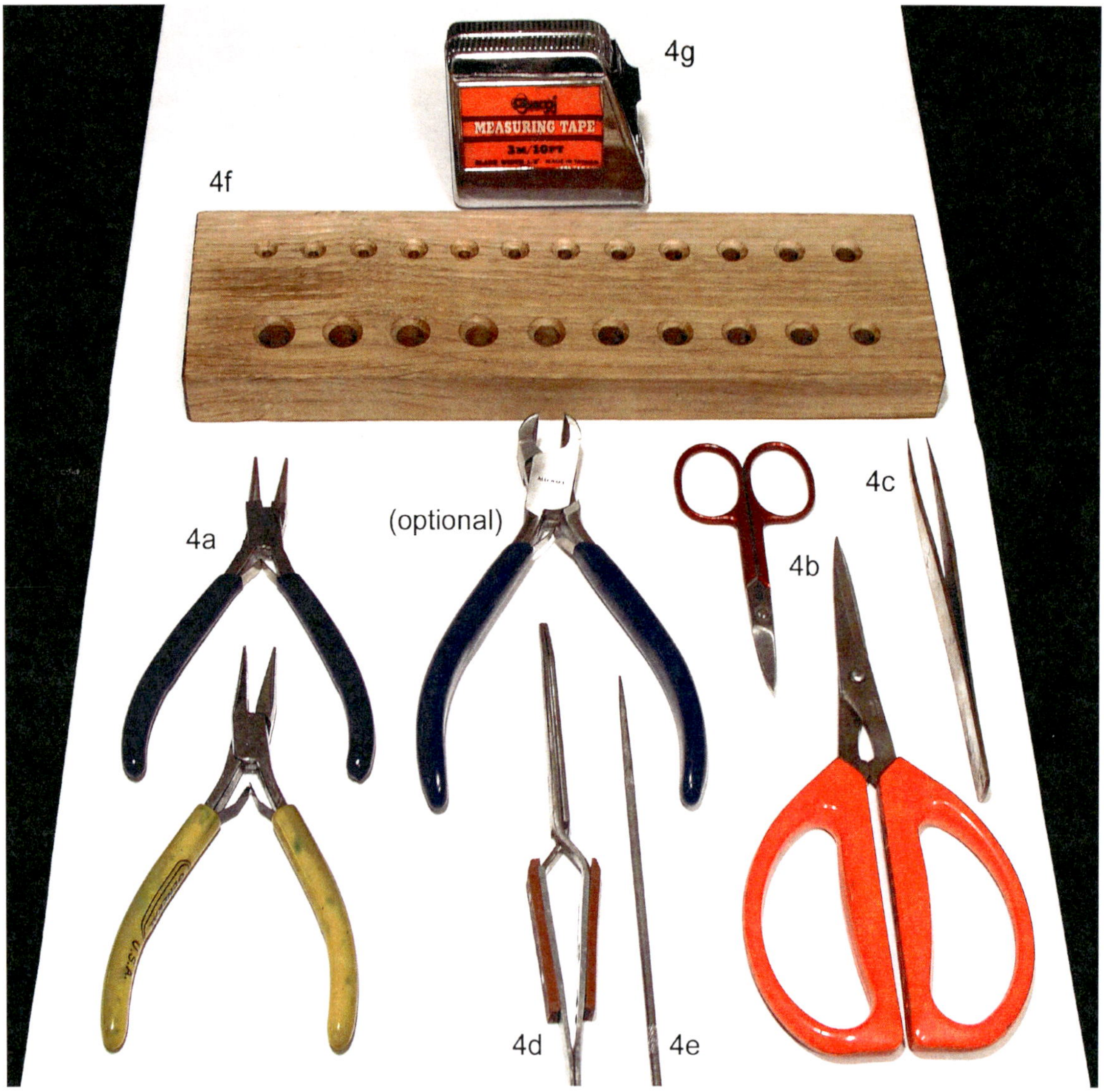

Figure 3

5. *(Figure 4)*

a. Stay-Brite flux and soldering kit. *(Low temperature solder)*

b. Blazer GB2001-Butane for soldering.

c. JAX Blackener for oxidizing.

d. Instant-Dip Silver Cleaner.

e. EXTRA Stay-Clean Flux

f. Solderite Board

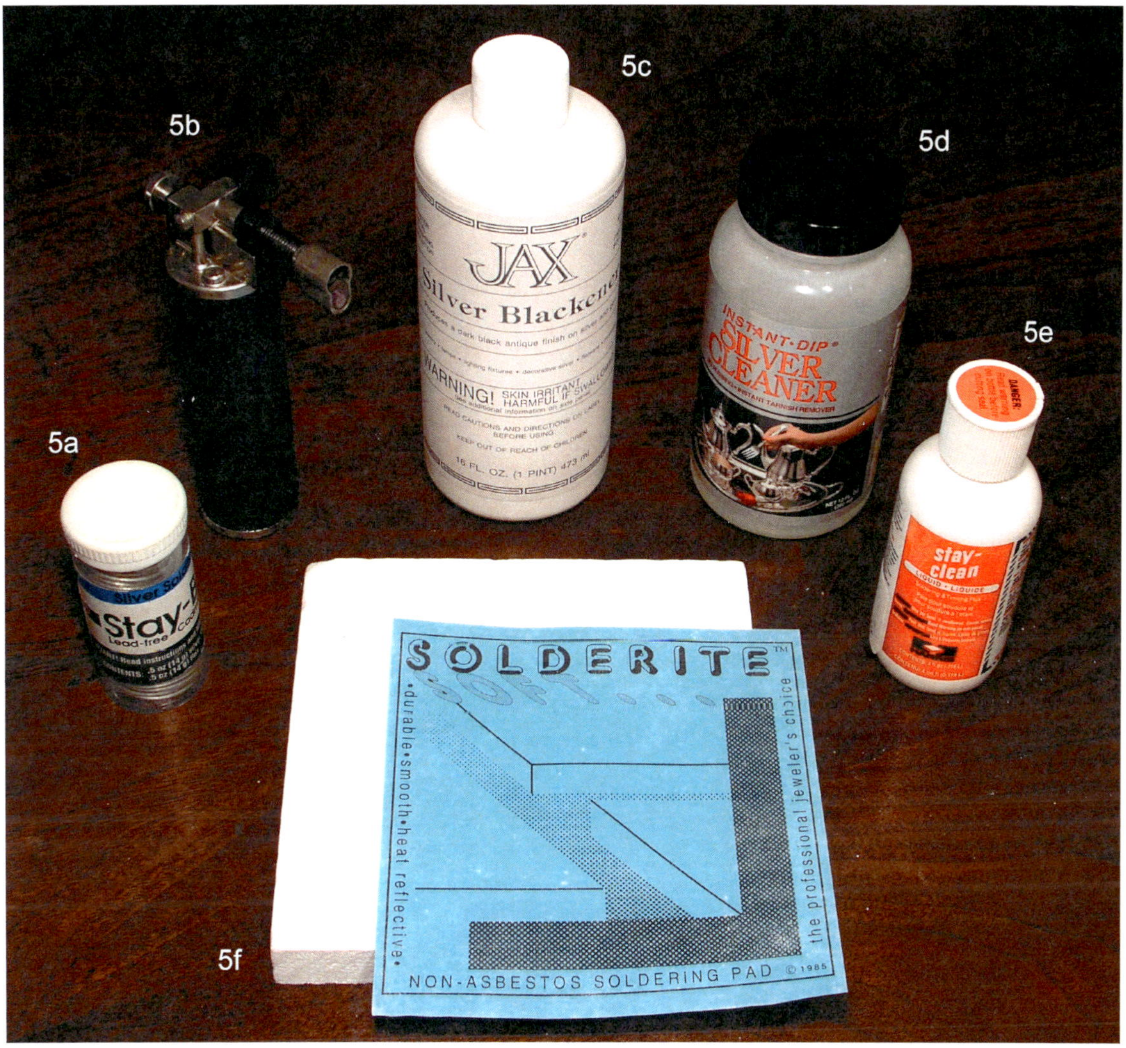

Figure 4

6. Other items not pictured:

a. 18K extreme easy for soldering fine gold wire to endcaps available from Precious Metals West. *(See Supply Source for details)*

b. Safety glasses

c. Safety mask

d. Opti-Lens Magnifying head piece

e. Tide Liquid (without bleach)

7. Optional items

a. Plastic Plate with sections

b. Small towel

c. Aluminum foil bowl

In order to master the techniques, it is best to start with the 5-prong wooden spool and work with 26- or 28-gauge craft wire.

II. STARTING YOUR WORK

A. Single Loop

This simple pattern will produce a single rope weave that can be easily tightened while producing a beautiful result.

Make a knot and put the end of wire through center of wooden spool.

Setup Step One

While turning your spool clockwise, loop the wire around all 5 cotter pins, going from inside to outside, counter clockwise. *(Inside means near the center hole.)*

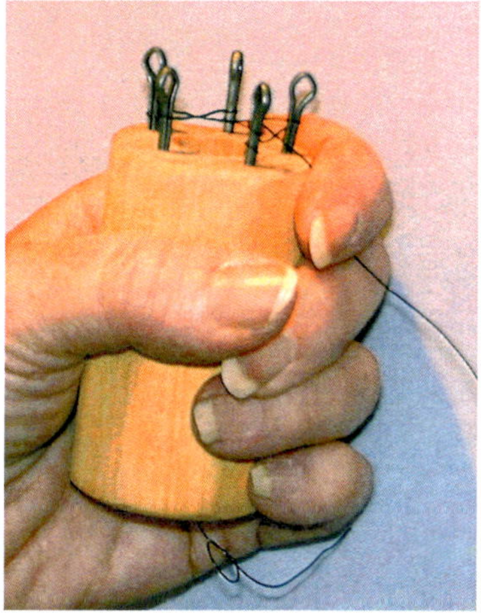

Single Stitch ready to loop

After you complete all 5-cotter pins and are back to the 1st position, take the next wire loop from the bottom and pull over the top loop.

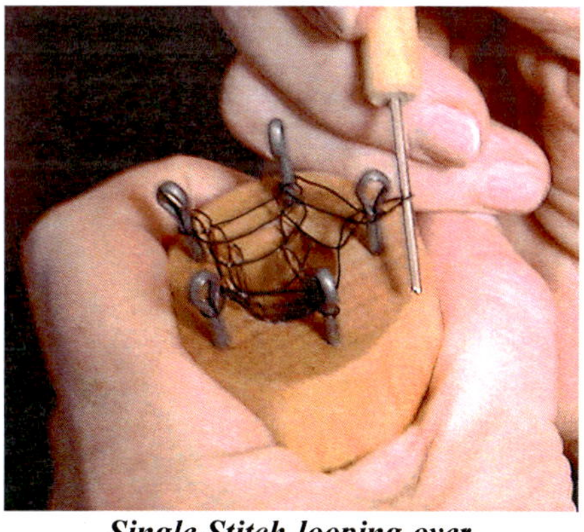

Single Stitch looping over

Always crochet at least 4 rows of loops without beads or pearls. This is called the LEAD. You will need this LEAD to secure an endcap and finish your work. *Important note:* Left-handed people should turn the spool ***counterclockwise*** and go around all 5-cotter pins ***clockwise.***

B. Double Loop

From inside to outside *twice* around, then pull bottom loop over the top two loops. My favorite pattern is the double loop. It produces a thick rope weave whereby glass beads and pearls appear to be suspended in space.

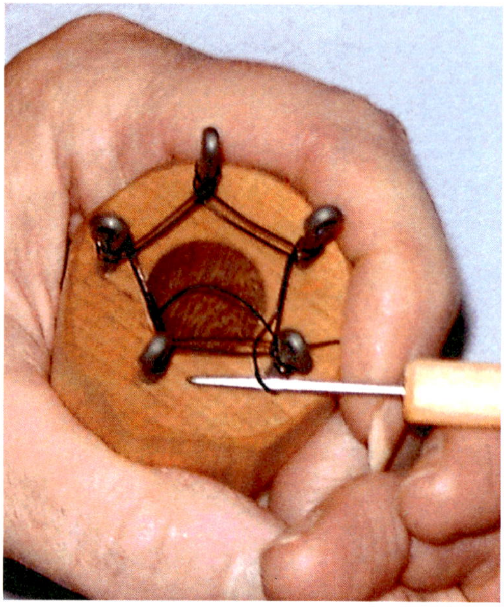

Double Stitch ready to loop over

C. Triple Loop

From inside to outside *three* times around, then pull bottom loop over the top three loops. A more advanced pattern which will be mastered quickly. The results are unusual and the pattern produces a thicker weave. The triple loop is stronger and is very effective for bracelets, too.

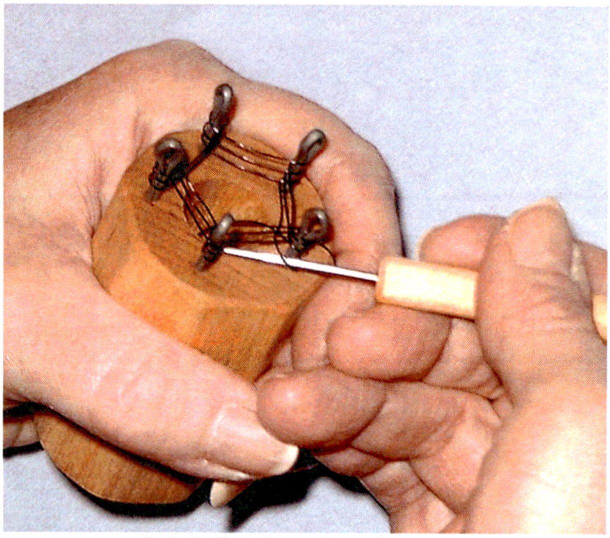

Triple Stitch ready to loop over

III. SNAKE PATTERN
(Also known as the Double Helix, DNA, or the Genome)

There are many varieties you can construct with this pattern, but for the sake of simplicity, let's begin with the basic concept.

For a 14" – 16" necklace, using 30-gauge fine silver wire, string 200-250 pearls, beads or crystals, no larger than 4mm in size. If you are using crystals, the rondelle shape (also referred to as bicone) works nicely.

As you progress in learning the technique, you may incorporate 5mm, 6mm or 8mm beads, crystals or pearls, keeping in mind that they must be able to go through the center of your wooden spool without crimping and squashing the beads, crystals or pearls.

Use a 5-prong wooden spool and string ***two different colors*** in a 3:1 ratio. For example: crystal, crystal, crystal, pearl. String all 200-250 crystals and pearls.

Using the double stitch go around at least four times without any crystals or pearls. This will provide a lead section for placement of an endcap and findings. *(See Chapter XXIII: How to End Your Work)*

After your lead is complete, start by placing a crystal between the first and second prong; second and third prong; third and fourth prong, and a pearl

The pattern looks like this:

Black Crystal and Pearl Snake Design

C = *Crystal*
P = *Pearl*
L = *Loop*

CCCPC
LLLLL
CCPCC
LLLLL
CPCCC
LLLLL
PCCCP
LLLLL
CCCPC
LLLLL
CCPCC
LLLLL
CPCCC
LLLLL

Using two different colors of crystals, without loops in between, you will get a tighter weave.

You can get a similar effect with the 4-prong wooden spool, but remember to reduce the pattern by one!

String 320 crystals of two different colors as shown in this Topaz-Faded Rose Crystal necklace. The results will reveal the beautiful snake pattern.

Topaz/Faded Rose Crystals Snake Design

TC *= Topaz Crystal*
FRC *= Faded Rose Crystal*

TC, FRC, FRC, TC
FRC, FRC, TC, FRC
FRC, TC, FRC, FRC
TC, FRC, FRC, TC

You may wish to string chips and pearls in this variation of the snake pattern. String 75 chips and 150 pearls, using the 4-prong spool and a double stitch, inserting the chips and pearls as follows:

Ch = Chip
P = Pearl
L = Loop

PPChP
LLLL
PChPP
LLLL
ChPPCh
LLLL
PPChP
LLLL
PChPP

Amethyst and Pearl Snake Design

IV. EAST/WEST – NORTH/SOUTH PATTERN WITH INNER WEAVE

To see the East/West–North/South pattern properly, it is important that a woven wire necklace without any crystals, pearls or beads be made before you start the pattern. This will give the necklace depth and the pearls can "sit" on the outside. Although you can make the necklace without an inner weave, the look is not as outstanding. *(See Chapter XIV Weave-in-Weave Pattern)*

a.

b.

c.

d.

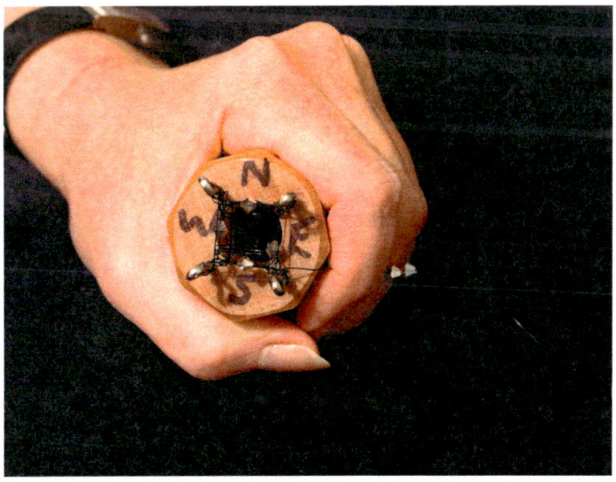

Photos ***a – d*** offered in black craft and silver crystals for instructional purposes. Follow this sequence exactly to achieve the East/West – North/South patten.

In fact, to make sure the pearls really stick out, I make two inner weaves! One weave with the 3-prong (double stitch), one with a 4-prong (double or triple stitch), then woven into the 5-prong (double or triple stitch), with the pearls. Each weave is woven into the other: 3-prong wooden spool with double stitch weave, woven into the 4-prong wooden spool with double or triple stitch weave. Henceforth, after the first two are complete, weave into the last 5-prong spool using a double or triple stitch with the crystals and pearls. This takes time, but the result is fantastic! *(See Page 38)*

Pearl and Fine Silver. Pattern: Triple Weave-in-Weave and East/West pattern on outside weave.

V. FLORETTE PATTERN

The Florette pattern is basically a necklace with sections of either the same or alternating colors. For example, you may want to have a combination of pearls and crystals or pearls, beads and crystals or just one color crystal or pearl.

For the basic 16" necklace string at least 240 crystals, pearls or beads onto 30-gauge fine silver. The florette can be made on either a 4-prong wooden spool (divided into groups of 8) or using a 5-prong wooden spool, divided into groups of 15. You may also use either a double or triple stitch.

If you use a single stitch you can create a flat design. After it is completed, press down on the necklace and draw it through your fingers. The necklace literally stretches out and appears to resemble swirls.

Now, let's get back to the basic florette pattern. Start on a 4-prong spool with a lead of four loops without crystals or pearls. Use the double stitch for this necklace. Two rows of crystals, two rows without anything, two rows with pearls, then repeat.

String all 240, using an 8 count:
8 crystals, then 8 pearls, 8 crystals, 8 pearls and so forth.

For the 5-prong spool string all 240, using a 15 count.
15 crystals, then 15 pearls, 15 crystals, 15 pearls.

Assuming you are using a 4-prong wooden spool the pattern is as follows:

Florette Gold Pearl and Crystal Necklace

C = Crystal
P = Pearl
L = Loop

CCCC
CCCC
LLLL
LLLL
PPPP
PPPP
LLLL
LLLL
CCCC
CCCC
and so on

VI. SOLDIER ROWS

Soldier rows is a pattern of all crystals, all beads or all pearls without any loops in between. Remember to use no more than 4mm sized crystals, beads or pearls in order to assure that the crystals, beads or pearls will not jam. If you are using 2mm, you probably can place two (2) of each between each prong. In order to visualize the **true** soldier row pattern you must use different colors for each row. Red, yellow, green and blue (RYGB, RYGB, RYGB, RYGB). At any rate, this pattern requires the stringing of at least 300-350 4mm crystals, on 30-gauge fine silver wire, in order to produce a 16" necklace.

If you want 18" or even 21" add fifty 4mm crystals for every inch. If you are working only with 3mm crystals, string double the amount.

Start again with a lead of four loops without anything. Using a 4-prong wooden spool the pattern is quite simple.

Soldier Rows Crystal Necklace

VII. CRYSTAL ROWS AND FACETED CRYSTAL DROPS PATTERN

Use 30-gauge fine silver wire or 18K gold wire on a 4-prong wooden spool, then string 253 4mm crystals and 22 crystal drops. This will produce a 16" necklace. String 11 4mm crystals and one drop and repeat for 22 sets, then the last 11 crystals will not have a drop (253 + 22 = 275). You must string in this **exact** order or your drop will not hang properly in one row.

When making a necklace with a drop pattern, use a 5½mm x 11mm crystal drop with the hole drilled through the top, which hangs like a teardrop, as opposed through the whole crystal, which does not hang. Anything larger will not fit through the hole in the middle of the wooden spool.

As always crochet four rows without any crystals for your lead. Using the double stitch the pattern will look like this:

C = Crystal
L = Loop
D = Drop

CCCC
LLLL
CCCC
LLLL
CCCD
LLLL
CCCC
LLLL
CCCC
LLLL
CCCD
and so on

Black AB Crystals – Drop Design in Gold

One final point, and a very important one – when you crochet the DROP, make sure it does not go inside the center of the hole, but is pushed on the outside of your necklace. It will then hang properly on the outside of your necklace as it emerges from the center of the wooden spool.

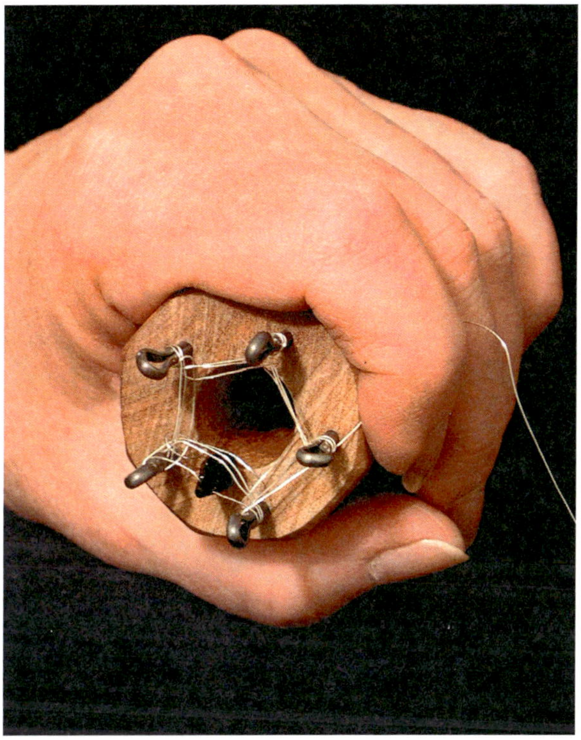

VIII. LARGE FLORETTE SECTIONS PATTERN

This pattern is an outgrowth of the original florette pattern, but is different in that there are no spaces separating the florettes. The florettes are also much larger.

Using a 4-prong wooden spool, string one set of **20 + three sets of 12,** each in a different colored crystal, totaling 336, as illustrated in the **Irish Combo** below (in green, grey, yellow and blue). This amount will easily make a 16"-18" necklace. Using a double stitch the pattern will look like this photo.

Start with a lead of four rows of loops without any crystals.

CCCC – 5 rows green crystal
CCCC – 3 rows grey crystal
CCCC – 3 rows yellow crystal
CCCC – 3 rows blue crystal

Irish Combo in Green, Gray, Yellow and Blue

IX. ALL-IN-ONE PATTERN

Another pattern similar to the Irish Combo is the All-in-One pattern which gives a rather spectacular effect.

Use a 4-prong wooden spool, string 350 4mm crystals of the **same** color on 30-gauge fine silver wire. Using the **double stitch only,** crochet all 350 crystals until complete, leaving no loops in between. Then, gently pull the necklace through a wooden draw plate to even it out. This makes a 16" necklace without the findings. When adding findings, the necklace becomes 17½ – 18" in length. If you wish to make a **choker,** string 320 crystals or less.

Point of information: The average choker is 13½" – 14"; a collar bone length necklace is 15" – 16". For a necklace below the collar bone, which works well over sweaters, you should make your necklace at least 18" in length.

18K Gold, Amethyst & Crystals Necklace and Bracelet

X. ZIG-ZAG PATTERN

This pattern is a slight variation of the "All-in-One" but the crystals and a combination of pearls and/or favorite beads are strung differently. As mentioned in the beginning, many of the patterns follow a mathematical configuration. For example:

Use a 4-prong wooden spool and string 250 4mm crystals and approximately 100 4mm peridots, with either 30-gauge fine silver or 30 gauge 18K gold wire. This will produce sets of 5:1 to one set of 5:2 every sixth time. (Not as complicated as it sounds.)

5 crystals to 1 peridot five times; then 5 crystals to 2 peridots once. Repeat until all 350 are strung. There are no loops in between, but you do make a lead of four without any crystals or peridots, as in all the patterns.

C = Crystal
P = Peridot

CCCC
CPCC
CCCP
CCCC
CPCC
CCCP
CCCC
CPCC
CCCP
PCCC
CCPC
(notice the zig-zag)

Peridot Bead and Topaz Crystal (actual length 18")

This will produce an 18" necklace. When pulled through a wooden draw plate and adding findings, the necklace should be about 21".

XI. CIRCULAR FLAT "CHOKER STYLE" PATTERN

The "Choker" flat pattern is a very popular style. This, too, can be done with the simple wooden spool. Inasmuch as the pattern is not an all-around each loop style, but utilizes only 3 prongs on a 4- or 5-prong wooden spool, it can be a bit tricky to master.

Using 30-gauge fine silver, craft wire or gold wire, double or triple stitch, go around each of the 3 prongs in a counter clockwise pattern, if you are right-handed; but clockwise if you are left-handed. As you work you must remember to press down with your wooden "pick" in a curved motion on the inside of the spool. For simplicity's sake, the first flat choker will not have any crystals, pearls or beads. It will look like this (on a 5-prong spool):

L = Loop
N = Nothing

LLL NN
LLL NN
LLL NN

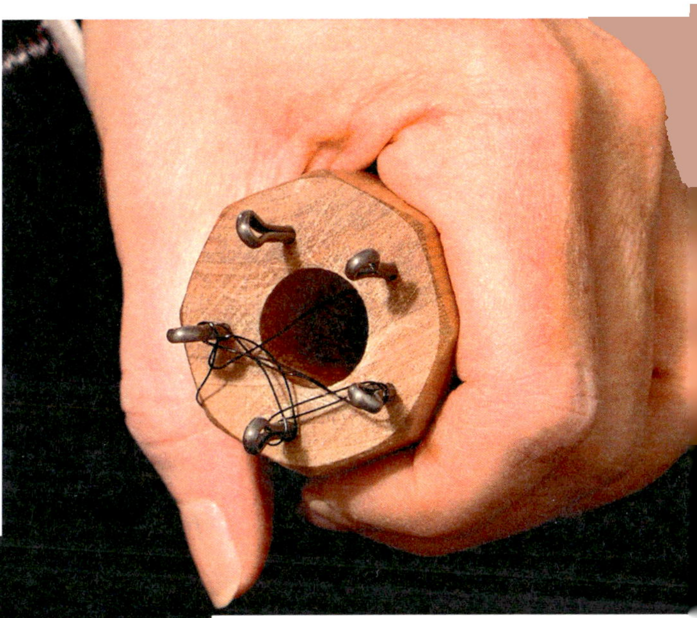

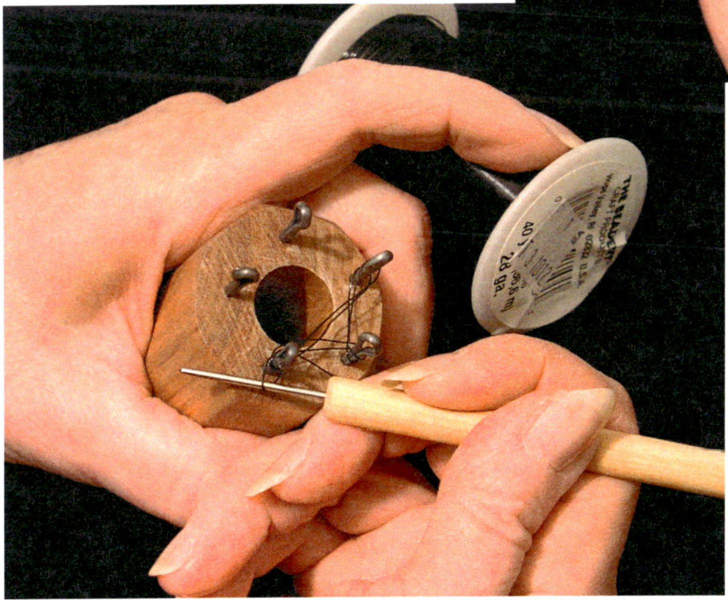

Loop between first and second cotter pin, and then second and third, and, finally, go across to the first cotter pin, skipping fourth and fifth cotter pins.

These are further examples of the flat Choker design in both black craft wire and fine silver wire.

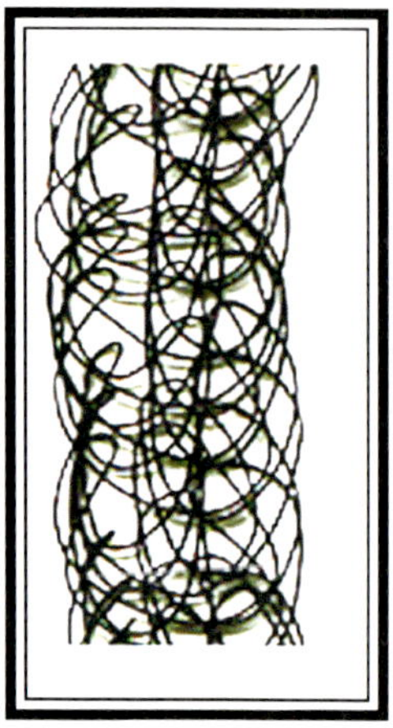

Flat Black Craft Wire Necklace

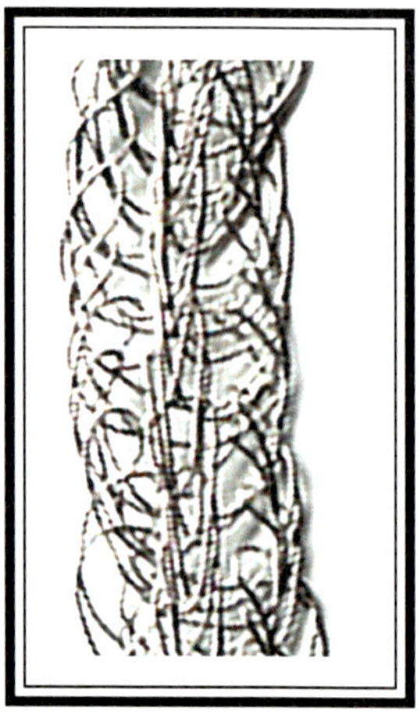

Flat Fine Silver Necklace

When you have perfected the pattern, add your crystals or pearls. This choker works well with small crystals, beads or pearls (only 2 or 3 mm). If you use larger crystals, beads or pearls, the pattern develops a very lumpy appearance and doesn't have that desirable airy quality. String only 60-80 2mm or 3mm pearls on your wire. Place the pearls in between the first and second, and second and third loops only. Use your 4-prong wooden spool.

Remember that nothing is on the fourth loop.

PPL
LLL
LLL
PPL
LLL
LLL
PPL

Flat Pink Pearl Craft Wire Necklace

A hands-on demonstration should help with this advanced pattern.

XII. HEAVY GAUGE WEAVE PATTERN

I also refer to this pattern as the elongated "wheat" style. You should use only fine silver in 24- or 26-gauge. Do not attempt this pattern with 22-gauge fine silver, because it is too difficult to loop over the cotter pins. If you wish to use 18K gold, use only 24- or 26-gauge.

This pattern does not call for any crystals, beads or pearls. It is just a weave that is gently pulled through a wooden draw plate for the "wheat" style. However, you may **choose not** to pull the weave through a draw plate and this will give you more of an airy, very springy appearance. I have completed many of these weaves in both styles.

Fine silver or gold is heavier when the gauge number is lower, so be sure you have at least one troy ounce for this pattern. Although splicing can be done, it is prudent to make certain that you have enough wire to complete the necklace.

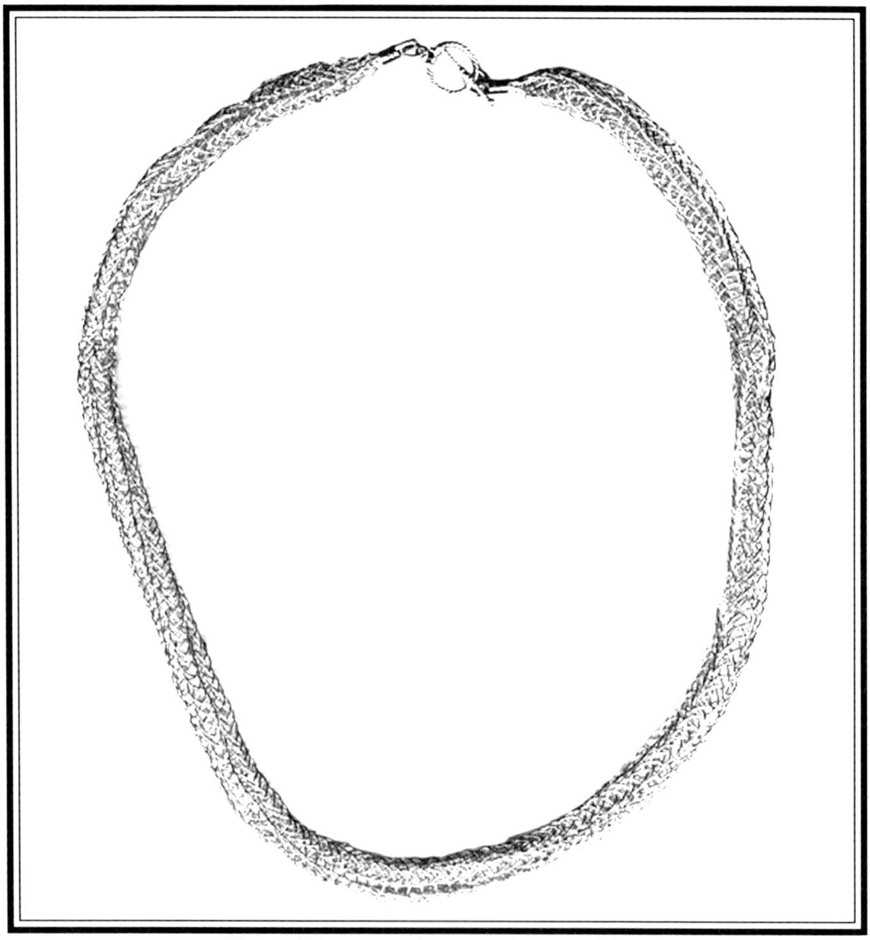

Heavy Weave 24-Gauge Silver Necklace

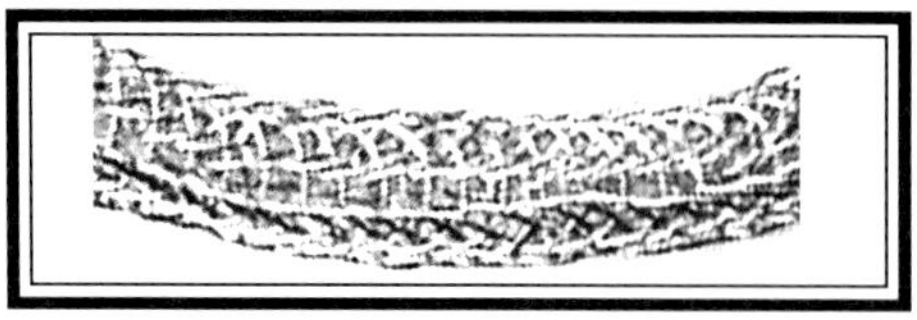

For a square design use the 4-prong wooden spool and do not pull through a wooden drawplate. The necklace in the photo below was slightly pulled through the drawplate and became rounder.

24-Gauge Fine Silver Choker

For a square-shaped smaller wheat-weave use the 4-prong wooden spool. This pattern requires the double stitch only. The single stitch is too flimsy and the triple stitch almost impossible to lift over the cotter pins.

LLLL or LLLLL
LLLL or LLLLL
and so on

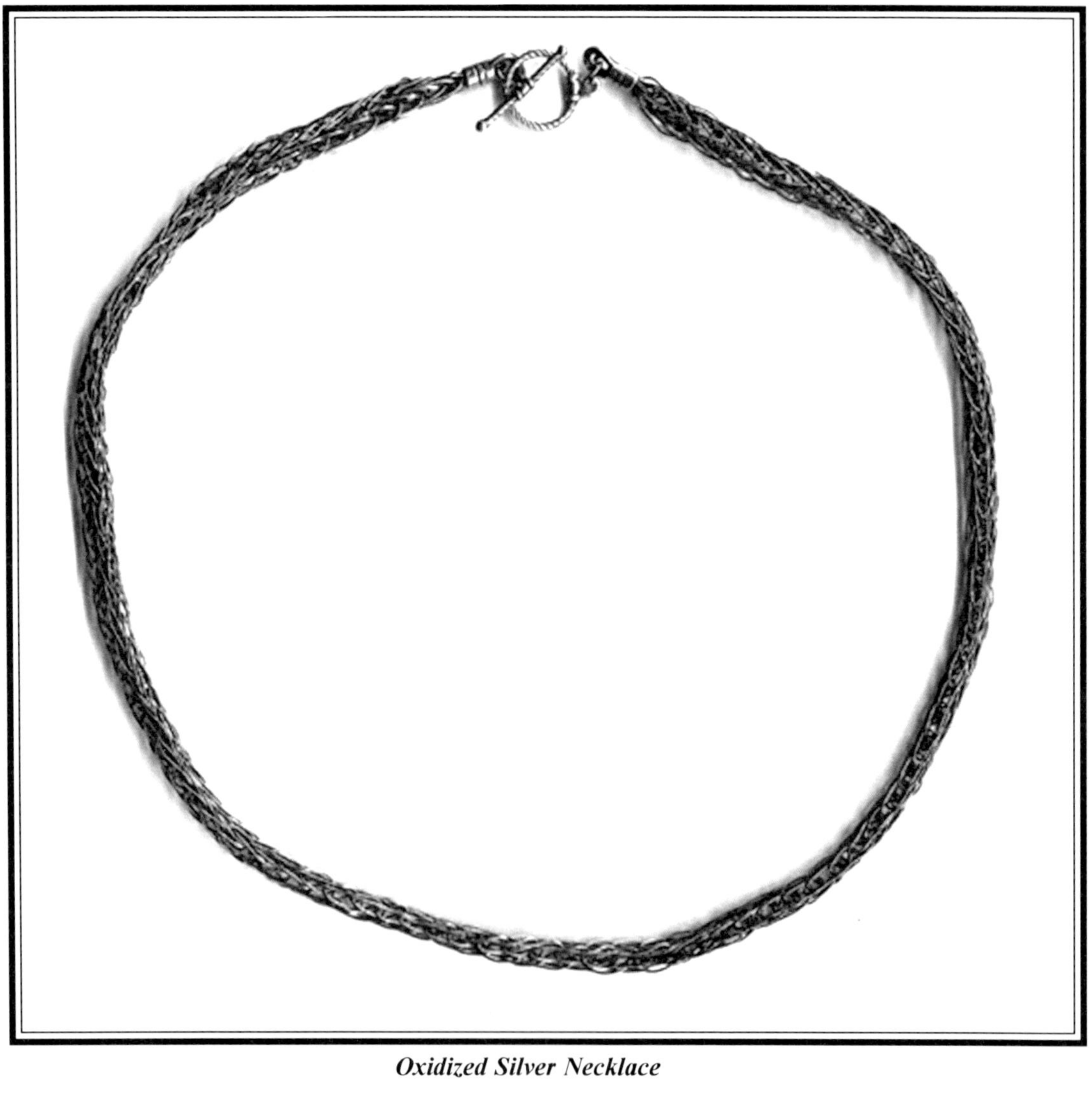

Oxidized Silver Necklace

When you achieve the length you desire, pull gently through the wooden draw plate until it becomes thinner. If you wish to make a 16"– 18" necklace, you only need to crochet 13½" – 14" because it will stretch an extra 1½" – 2", when you pull it through the draw plate. After adding your findings, you may end up with a necklace of 17" – 18" in length. In this example I have oxidized the necklace with Jax Blackener *(Refer to List of Materials).*

Point to remember: Don't stress the metal when putting through the draw plate or it will curl.

XIII. CRAZY FOUR "X" PATTERN

This is a very advanced technique that should not be attempted until mastery of all other patterns. It requires crocheting with two spools of metal or craft wire at one time on the same 4-prong wooden spool. Once completed, the pattern appears to fan out and is very unusual. I prefer to use two different metals, one in silver and one in gold. This will bring out the pattern rather strikingly.

You should use a heavier gauge wire for this pattern. Use 26 gauge fine silver and 26 gauge 18K gold. I also insert semi-precious stones in 4-5mm for the central row. String 75 stones on the fine silver and 75 stones on the 18K gold.

The pattern looks like this: First – loop 1 and 3 using the fine silver; on loops 2 and 4 use the 18K gold.

- **Loop in order,** to form an "X" pattern as you proceed.
- Loop four rows of silver and four rows of gold, without any stones.
- Then, between loops 1 and 3, place a semi-precious stone.
- Between loops 2 and 4, place another semi-precious stone.

It can be the same color or two different colored stones, which is a matter of taste.

Using the double stitch:

S = Silver
G = Gold

Loop 1 (S) go across to loop 3 (S)
Loop 2 (G) go across to loop 4 (G)

Rotate your wooden spool clockwise as you work (counter clockwise for left-handed people).

Between loops 1 and 3, using your silver spool, place your semi-precious stone. Between loops 2 and 4, using your gold spool, place your semi-precious stone.

Silver loop, stone, silver loop
Gold loop, stone, gold loop

Then, do a row without any stones, and continue until all 150 semi-precious stones are inserted, finish with four rows without any stones. Pinch the ends and place your findings. Watching this technique demonstrated in person will assist you in mastering the pattern.

You may wish to practice and experiment with two different colors of craft wire and use crystals or pearls. The first one I completed was this black craft wire and silver wire with 4mm African Jade for the center. You can also do the triple stitch with this pattern, but use 28-gauge wire in lieu of 26-gauge to prevent tangling.

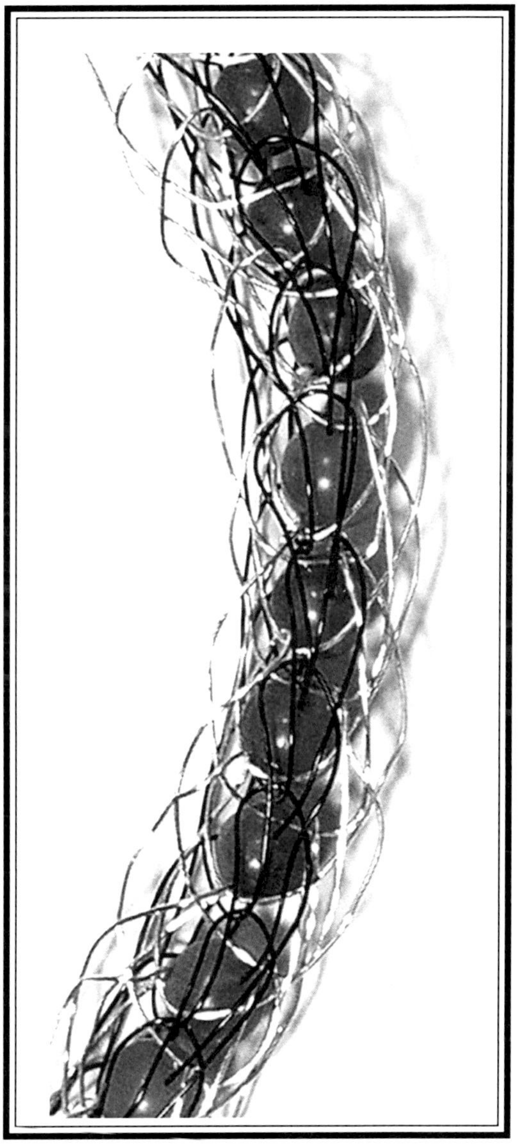

African Jade Necklace – Crazy Four "X"

XIV. WEAVE-IN-WEAVE PATTERN

Although discussed briefly in the East/West design segment, the weave-in-weave pattern has many, many variations. The basic pattern can have one or two weaves inserted into outer weaves of various gauges and colors. You can use 30-gauge wire with a triple or double stitch for your inner chamber(s). Please keep in mind that the inner weave must be able to fit into the hole of the wooden spool when crocheting. It is important to insert your inner weave after about 2½" of your outer weave has been completed, otherwise you will have a difficult time trying to insert it.

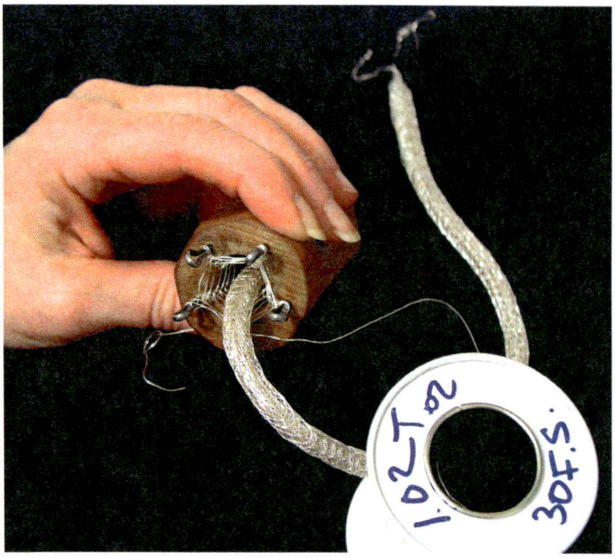

Wait until you have completed about 2"–2½" of your outer weave, then feed the inner weave into the outer weave and tie the end of the first weave to the end of the outer weave. By tying these ends together slippage will be prevented. You will be able to pull both through the wooden spool without the inner weave falling out. As you work your outer pattern, keep feeding the inner weave through the center of your spool.

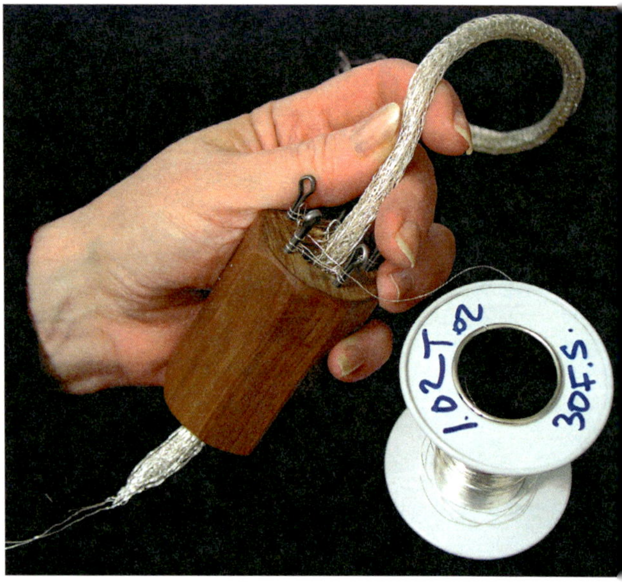

First, make an inner weave with 30-gauge fine silver wire, on a 3- or 4-prong wooden spool, using a triple stitch. If the weave is too thick, pull it through a wooden draw plate. In this way you will be able to feed this weave into the next weave. Then, with 30-gauge fine silver wire, using a 4-prong wooden spool, feed 200-250 4mm pearls or a combination of crystals and pearls. Either string all one color, or two and two in your desired color scheme. *Remember, as always, make a lead going around four times without any crystals and pearls.*

Combination of Crystals/Pearls
CLCL
LLLL
LPLP
LLLL
CLCL
LLLL
LPLP

After you have completed two inner weaves, you are ready to insert them into your grey pearl outer weave. String 250 4mm grey pearls on 30-gauge fine silver. Using a double stitch and a 4-prong wooden spool, begin weaving the pearls as follows *(do your lead of 4 rounds without anything)*:

All One-Color Pearls
P = Pearl
L = Loop
PLPL
LLLL
LPLP
LLLL
PLPL
LLLL
LPLP

Pearl and Fine Silver Necklace/ Triple Weave-in-Weave

Another version of the weave-in-weave is to use 18K gold, 30-gauge wire with a double stitch on a 4-prong spool. Pull it through a wooden draw plate and then make another triple stitch weave, using the same 4-prong spool and insert the first weave into the second weave. When this is accomplished, use a 5-prong spool with a triple stitch, inserting the first two weave-in-weaves into the third weave. This produces the gorgeous golden, airy weave-in-weave-in weave!

18K Gold Necklace Weave-in-Weave-in-Weave

This is an example of a weave-in-weave-in-weave bracelet.

18K Gold Bracelet

XV. LENI'S CHIPS PATTERN

I named this pattern after a talented jewelry designer, Leni Fuhrman. I taught Leni the technique of crocheting and weaving and she developed this gorgeous pattern.

Chips in different stones are very difficult to work with because of the variation in sizes and shapes. Chips have uneven edges, points and curves and the size usually ranges from 4mm to 7mm. They can also be tumble polished or rough and unpolished. I have worked with both. Because of the irregularity of the shape of the stone, the effect of the finished piece is quite unusual.

Using 30-gauge fine silver on a 4-prong wooden spool and a double stitch, string 150–200 chips in a pattern of 2:1 in two different colors or all in the same color. Because of the density and weight of the chips, crochet a lead of six rows to anchor the silver thread at each end. I used 5mm mother-of-pearl and black onyx chips as follows:

Mch = Mother-of-Pearl chip
Bch = Black Onyx chip
L = Loop
MchMchBchMch
LLLL
MchBchMchMch
LLLL
BchMchMchBch

If you cannot push the chips through the opening, loop over only three prongs. The necklace is airier, but beautiful. You might consider making two loops in between of just silver without chips.

You may even use 4 prongs on the 5-prong wooden spool.

The nicest thing about this pattern is that you can utilize many spectacular semi-precious chips in lapis lazuli, peridot, coral, onyx, carnelian, emeralds, rubies, in the most imaginative, creative ways. The cost of these semi-precious chips, compared to faceted or round stones, is very economical.

Leni's Black and White Chips Necklace

XVI. CRAFT WIRE PATTERNS

Craft wire is very flexible and can be purchased in a variety of colors. Navy blue, green, copper, silver colored, black (my favorite), purple and red. The lowest gauge is 24 and the highest is 32. Inasmuch as 32-gauge is unavailable in fine silver or gold, some of the patterns that can be achieved with this very thin thread are quite beautiful. The cost of craft wire is also relatively low. Most craft wire is made from copper wire that is coated in a malleable shiny plastic. (See Chapter IX All-In-One Pattern)

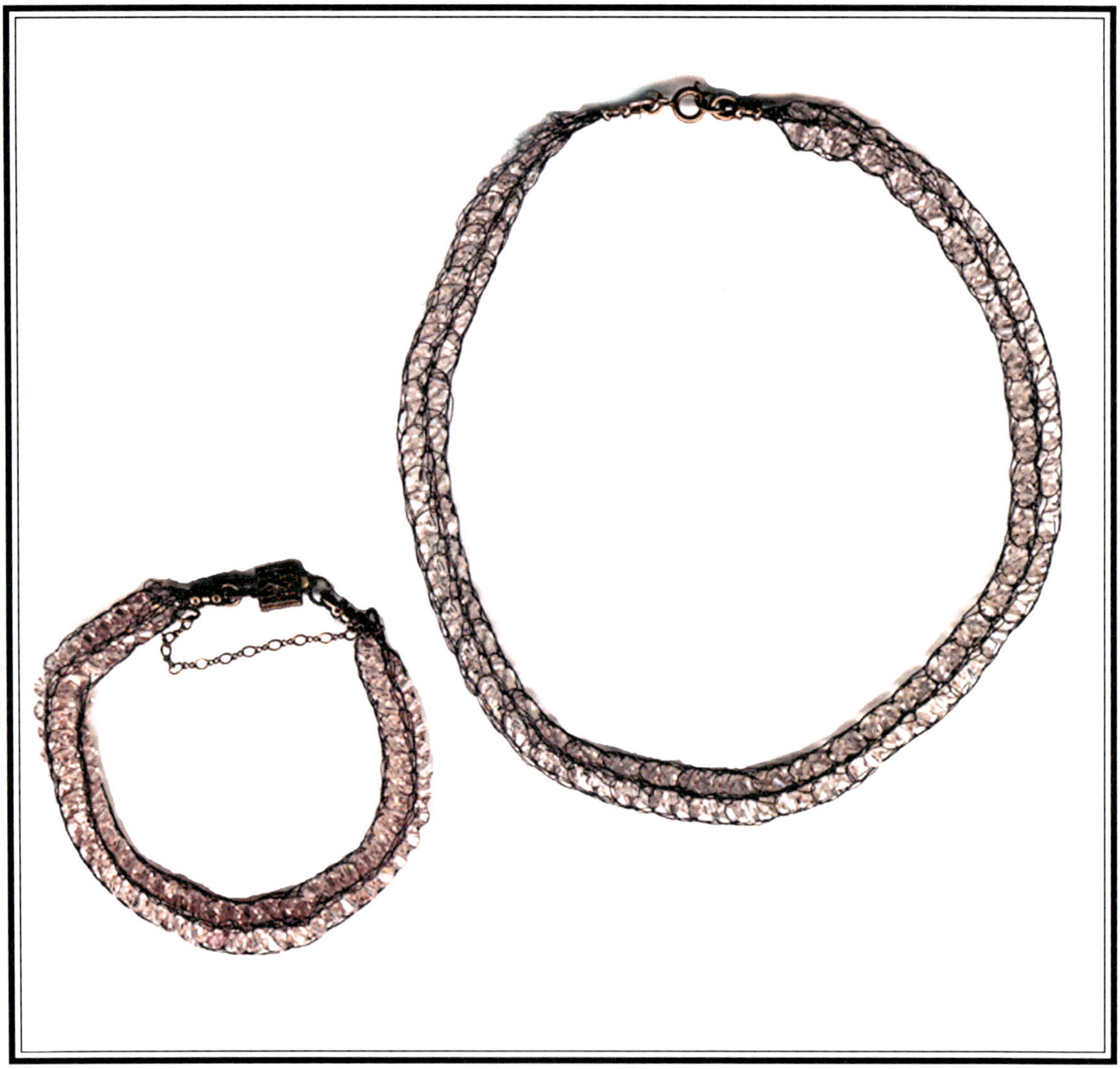

Black Craft Wire Bracelet and Necklace with Pink Crystals

Using Black 32-gauge craft wire you will achieve a beautiful lacy look for a **flat choker.** Working with a 4- or 5-prong wooden spool, you can thread a 4-5mm pearl, or a semi-precious stone or without any pearl or stone. As previously discussed in the detailed explanation of the **flat pattern**, use only 3 prongs of a 4- or 5-prong spool. The pattern is as follows:

> LLL *(4 times as your lead)*
> L *(place a pearl between #1 and #2 prong)*
> L *(place a pearl between #2 and #3 prong)*
> *Quarter turn clockwise and start again at the first prong.*

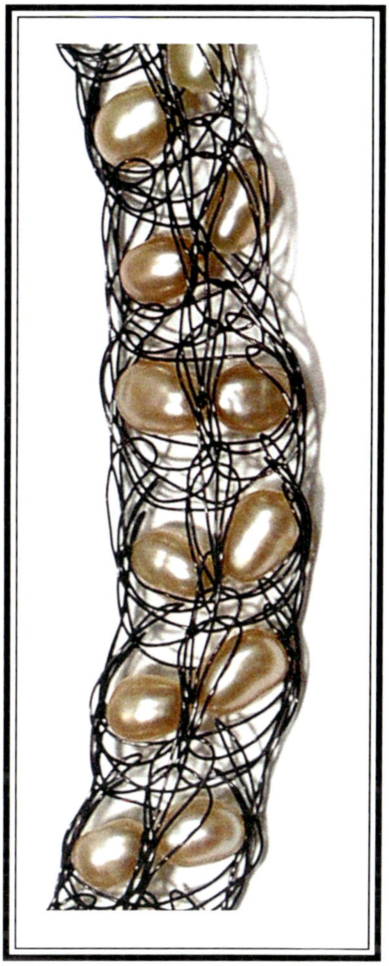

Black Craft Wire with Pink Pearls

If you wish to make the choker wider, use 4 prongs on a 5-prong spool. You may also **sew** two or three chokers together, using the craft thread and a basting stitch. Simply thread the 32 gauge black craft wire through a needle, (use one with a large eye opening). Craft needles for crocheting are also available.

The results are a choker with four or six rows of pearls in lieu of only two rows of pearls. The only difficult part is placing a proper finding on each end. I use a bayonet-style finding. This has room for attaching two, three or four strands on an elongated tube. Sounds complicated, but it is not. You can purchase this bayonet-style finding at Myron Tobak or Metalliferous *(see Supply Source)*. Just remember to add a jump ring without an endcap (looks too bulky with the endcap) and oxidize it to match the black craft wire.

XVII. WEAVE WITH A COIL

This is an advanced pattern that has a coiled inner chamber inserted into the woven pattern, which greatly enhances the look of your weave, making it stronger and more flexible. You can prepare your coil utilizing the "coiling gizmo," available at Metalliferous in New York City or you can make the coil using a small dowel. I find the coiling gizmo very easy to use and relatively inexpensive.

To make a 15" choker: Using 24-gauge fine silver, coil at least 13½" as evenly as possible. Do not pull the coil, just leave it nice and even.

Using a 4-prong wooden spool, double stitch, begin your weave. After you have woven about 2½"-3" of your outer weave, insert the prepared coil into the center of the spool and tie the inner coil to the tail of the outer weave. Sounds complicated, but it is very simple.

When you have woven 13½", squeeze each end of the choker tightly to ensure that the inner coil does not wiggle. Finish the choker with heavy (6mm opening) endcaps and handmade or commercial findings.

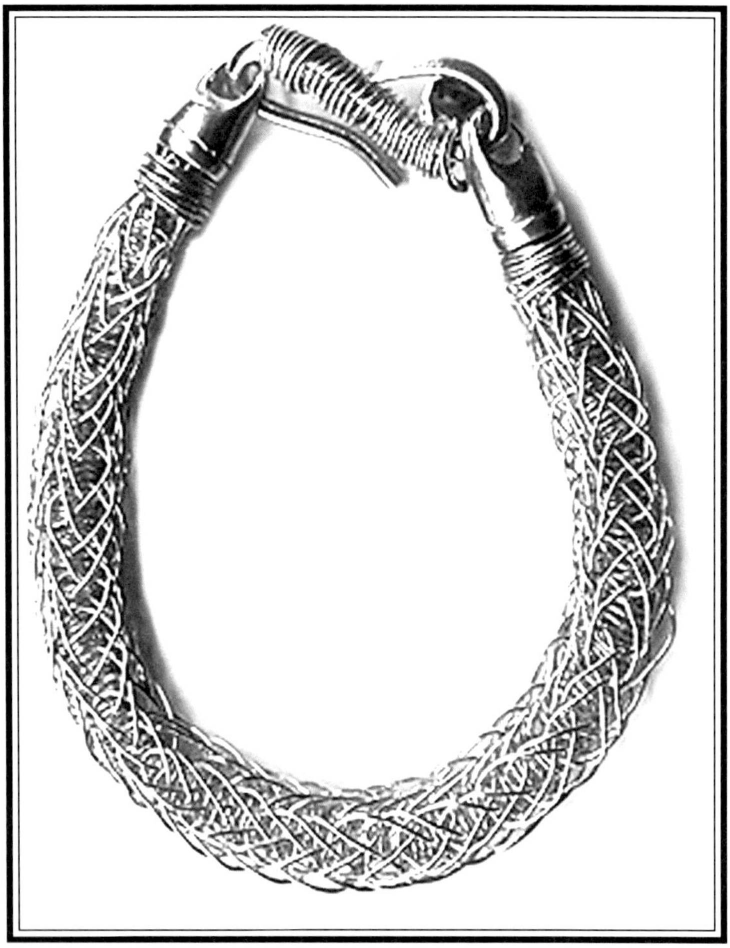

Silver Choker

To make a 15" choker with crystals, pearls, drops or fancy semi-precious stones, use the following pattern:

First, make your inner coil and have it ready. Then, string 224 crystals or pearls; 14 drops or semi-precious stones *(no bigger than 5mm)* onto your wire. As always, do four rows for your lead. When using drops, string them in a pattern of 11 to 1.

L = Loop
C = Crystal
D = Drops

CCCC
LLLL
CCCC
LLLL
CCCD
LLLL
CCCC
LLLL
CCCC
LLLL
CCCD
LLLL
CCCC
LLLL
CCCC
LLLL
CCCD
and so forth

Blue Crystal Drop Necklace with Inner Coil

XVIII. BRACELETS

You can vary the coil pattern by using 18K gold, craft or copper wire. With 18K gold use 26-gauge wire. 18K gold is not as soft as fine silver; it's harder to work into a pretty weave. In any case let your imagination run wild. For this bracelet I made an 18K gold, 26-gauge inner coil and used 18K gold 30-gauge wire with sapphire beads on the outside in a more random design.

18K Gold Weave with Coil and Sapphire

Most of the necklaces described in this book can be made smaller, and hence become a bracelet.

Bracelet lengths vary, depending on the wrist and whether the person wants a loose or tight fit. Average length is 7–7½", about half of a choker. When preparing a 7" bracelet, weave about 5½"–6" only, since the findings will extend the bracelet to the desired 7" length.

18K Gold Triple Weave-in-Weave with Agates

Another important point to remember is that bracelets must, *and I emphasize must,* be bound with a strong wire or a crimped endcap on each end. The reason for this is that bracelets are subject to much more pulling, twisting and jarring. *(See Chapter XXIV – How to End Your Work.)*

XIX. EARRINGS

A. WREATHS

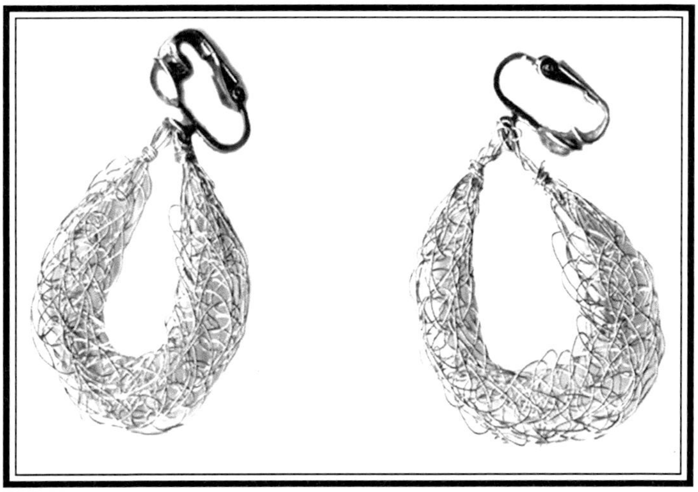

A. Silver Wreath Earrings

Using 24, 26, 28, or 30-gauge fine silver, a double or triple stitch, crochet 1½" – 2" with a 4- or 5-prong wooden spool. You may also use 18K gold or your favorite craft wire as well. After you have crocheted approximately 2", cast off and join the two ends with a jump ring. This gives the wreath the circular appearance.

Attach to an earring finding such as a French hook, post, lever back type or clip. Using your favorite crystals, pearls or semi-precious stones is another option. When using stones, crystals or pearls, make sure that they are no larger than 4mm.

B. WREATHS WITH A DROP

B. Silver Wreath Earrings with Green Crystal Drop

This is a variation of the wreaths and is very attractive, especially during the winter holidays. The simple technique is to add a 5½mm x 11mm crystal drop to the inner part of the wreath. Make sure your drop is drilled across the top of the crystal.

After you have joined the two ends of the wreath with your jump ring, add the drop to the jump ring before closing and securing it to the earring finding. Just make sure that the wire used fits through the opening of the stone. If it does not, you may have to use a thinner gauge jump ring or make your own with wire. Another great look is to use a pretty pearl, or semi-precious stone hanging from the center of the wreath.

C. FLAT WREATHS

This earring design was discovered by accident. After completing a plain 30-gauge fine silver wreath, I dropped it on the floor and, inadvertently, I stepped on it, but liked the look. So I made another earring to match. When I used a heavier 24-gauge fine silver wire, I placed the earring between two steel blocks to achieve a flatter look. I do not recommend flattening when there are stones inserted into the design! You may even flatten the earring by squeezing it between your fingers or palms of your hands.

C. Silver Flat Wreath Earrings

D. BIRD CAGES AND BELLS

This pattern has only 15 rows of loops and is done on either a 4- or 5-prong wooden spool with 18K wire, using a double stitch. Start with a lead of 4 rows without any crystals, then add 5 rows with crystals, and finish by weaving 4 rows without crystals. After casting off, close and crimp only one end of the earring with a jump ring and attach an earring finding. For the BELL design just pinch the open end upwards making it apear to look like a skirt.

D. 18K Gold Bird Cage Earrings with Amethysts

E. Silver Flat Design Earrings with Beads

E. FLAT DESIGN WITH BEADS

In order to perfect this design, use the 3 loops on a 4- or 5-prong wooden spool. (*See the description for the FLAT design on necklaces.*) Do not try this with a very heavy gauge. Using 30- or 28-gauge fine silver, string about 100 seed beads and place seed beads randomly in between each loop. After casting off, flatten the earring between your fingers, wrap extra wire to secure the top of each earring and add a jump ring to your earring finding.

F. EARRING WRAPS

When I was concentrating on refining the skills for producing *Bird Cage* and *Wreath Earrings*, I wanted to create a design that is both modern and easy to wear. After perusing fashion magazines, I noticed that women appeared to prefer round earrings in a variety of sizes. I bought some plain round silver earrings and began wrapping them with 26-gauge fine silver. I made them with one wrap, simple but not unusual. Then I made them with a wrap in one direction and a second wrap in the opposite direction. Nice, but not spectacular. I decided that in order for the earrings to have some pizzazz they needed a *third* row. Hence, my triple wrapped earrings! For demonstration purposes this example shows a wrap with nine crystals.

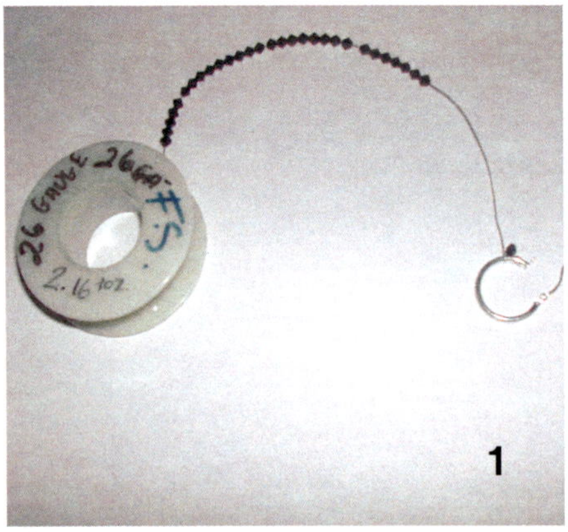

1

2

Start of Second Wrap

3

4

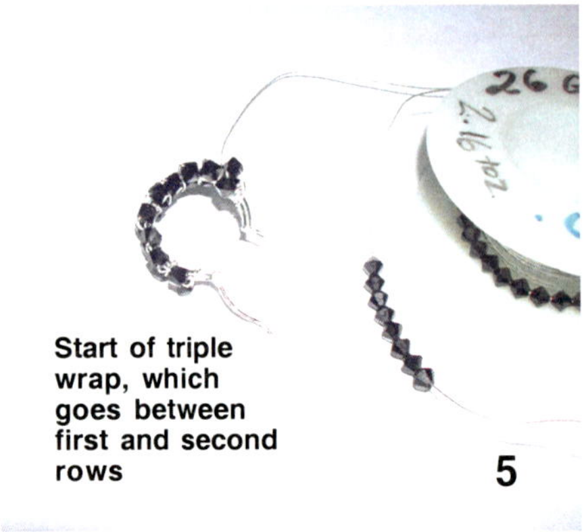

Start of triple wrap, which goes between first and second rows

5

6

They are a huge success! I make them in five different sizes. Plain, round earrings can be purchased in many jewelry supply stores.

10mm (tiny)
15mm (medium small)
20mm (medium large)
24mm (large)
28mm (extra large)

There are special codes I use in order to dfferentiate between the sizes.

Special Codes:

A. 2 Rows 6	(too tiny to make three rows)	10mm
B. 3 Rows 8	(medium small)	15mm
C. 3 Rows 11	(medium large)	20mm
D. 3 Rows 13	(large)	24mm
E. 3 Rows 16	(extra large)	28mm

For example: If a person likes only very tiny earrings, I make them in 10mm, using 2 Rows 6; for a medium small I make them in 15mm, 3 Rows 8 and so forth.

I only use **26 gauge fine silver** because through trial and error I found that 28 gauge was too fragile and the 24 gauge was too heavy looking.

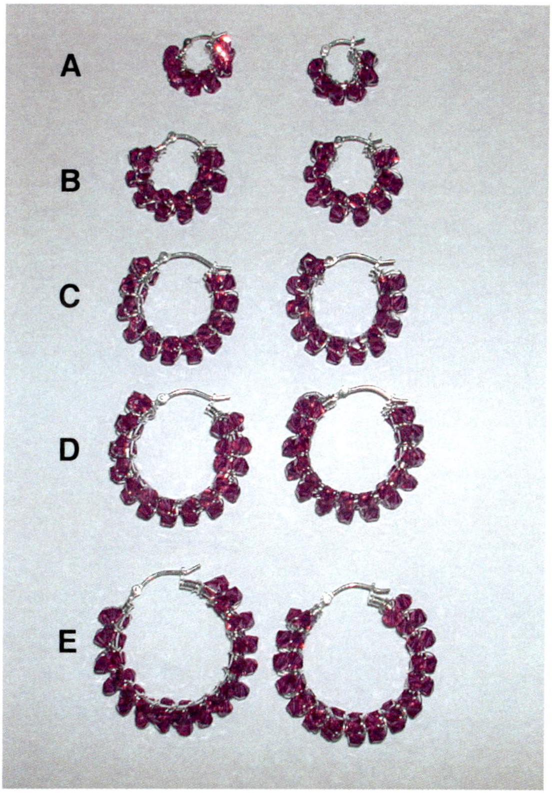

G. WOVEN ROUND EARRING ENHANCEMENT

A very glamorous addition to your woven necklaces is the woven round earring. I use heavier fine silver wire to create this new look. Using the 4-prong spool with 26-gauge fine silver wire and the double stitch, the following method is applied.

Small Round earring: **1.** For a small round woven earring you must go around 10 times on your 4-prong spool. **2.** Then, cast off and tightly tie each end. Use your hands to roll the earring as you would for pretzel dough. When this is completed, pull the earring through a wooden draw plate. Now you are ready to close up the ends. **3.** Join each end together to make a circle. You will notice that there is some extra wire on each end. I use this to make the finished round loop and add a jump ring to attach to an earring finding.

1.

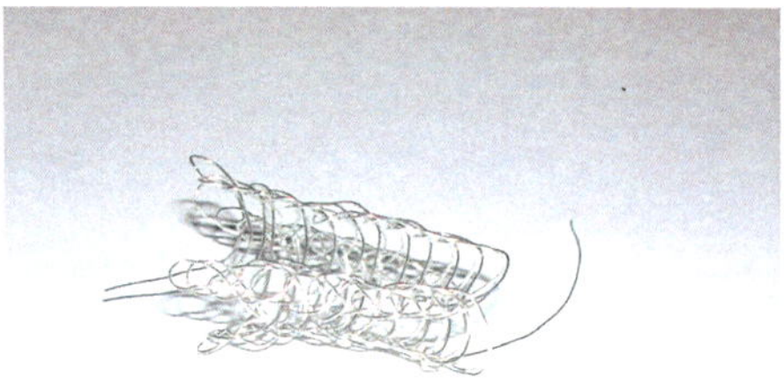

2.

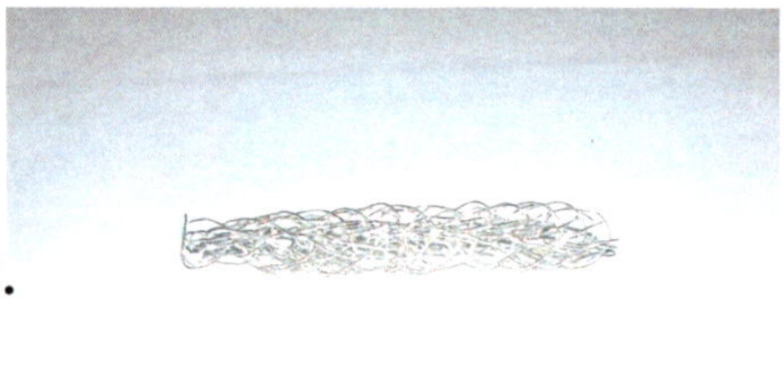

3.

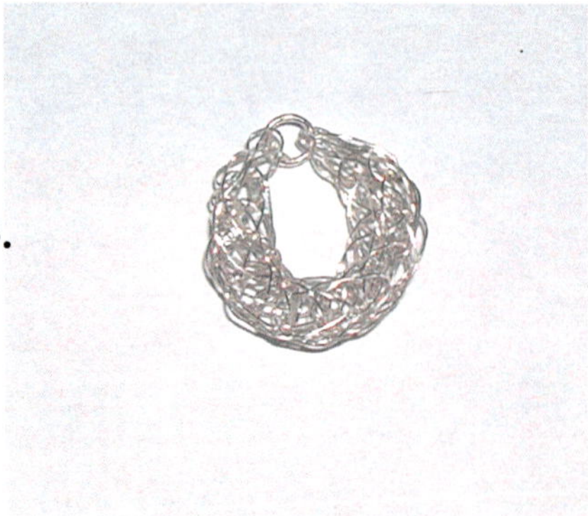

Medium Round woven earrings are done exactly as the small round, but it requires 15 rows for each earring.

Large Round woven earrings are made in the same manner, but requires 20 rows for each earring.

One way to keep count of how many rows you have made is to use the "PENNY" method. I place 10 pennies on the table and after I complete each row I shift a penny into a finished pile. Do the same for the medium and large as indicated below. It's simple, but it works!

10 pennies = small
15 pennies = medium
20 pennies = large

One more way to use this method and achieve the "new linear look" is not to tie the earring into a circle, but just leave it long. Below is an example of the linear earring with a twist and a crystal drop added for drama.

XX. LEATHER WEAVES

A very popular look these days are leather chokers. These designs are easy to master. Working with 1.5mm Greek black leather, weave about 13" of leather, using a **single** stitch and a 3-prong wooden spool. Then, when you add findings, the choker will be about 14½" long. This is the perfect size for the average lady's choker.

Black Leather and Olive Leather Necklaces

ENDCAPS AND EPOXY

Endcaps come in a variety of sizes and shapes. Some can be crimped to close a necklace; others soldered. To accomodate the leather weaves, the endcap must have at least a 3.5mm opening. Endcaps for leather pieces can be secured with epoxy. Just squeeze epoxy inside the endcap and place it at each end of the piece.

I prefer the 30-minute 2-Ton Epoxy made by Devcon, but others might work as well. This epoxy is available in most hardware stores, craft shops and jewelry supply outlets.

A SQUARE PATTERN

The same single stitch is used for this pattern, but use a 5-prong wooden spool. The leather should be slightly thinner, too. I recommend using 1.2mm Greek black leather cord. This is not the standard size, but can be ordered through jewelry supply stores and leather supply outlets.

Black Leather 5-Prong Necklace with Coil End Wrap

Because the necklace will be wider and square shaped, you must use an endcap that has at least a 4.5mm opening.

Since this size endcap is difficult to find, it is suggested that you use 16–18-gauge silver wire instead. In a circular pattern wrap around each end six or seven times, leaving one end open to use as a jump ring. *One important point:* tie the end of the leather with a big knot that will not pull through the 16-18-gauge silver wire, before you begin the circular pattern. To assure that nothing unravels, I secure this spiral, circular wire endcap with epoxy as well.

Leather is available in many colors – brown, red, green, gold, silver, etc. Black, however, appears to be the most popular. When I work in a color other than black, I apply an acrylic wax coating to the colored leather after it is woven. *Future* is the brand name of the acrylic wax I use; available in most supermarkets.

The reason I use the wax is that colored leathers, with the exception of black, tend to scrape off when pulling through the wooden spool.

You can also create bracelets using the same patterns and techniques as described above.

XXI. FILIGREE

This pattern was derived quite accidentally. As in many creative projects, sometimes an error can produce a positive result. When redesigning a leather necklace with wire wrapped around, I pulled the wrap from the leather and it twisted into a beautiful design. It suddenly had a gossamer-like appearance and resembled a delicately made filigree necklace. Here's how it was produced:

Crochet an 18"–21" length of black leather, using the 3-prong wooden spool. This will be the center insertion for the filigree pattern. The next step is to crochet the outer weave in fine silver or 18K gold. Using a 4-prong wooden spool, with a triple stitch, crochet either the silver or 18K gold 30-gauge wire. When you have completed 2½", insert the black leather into the wooden spool and continue crocheting until you reach the desired length. As an example – if you have an 18" black leather piece for the insertion, this will make either a 15" or 16" necklace. Remember to always allow 2 to 3 inches of slack for the twist.

After you make the necklace and have cast off, gently twist the outer layer of wire around the black leather in one direction and let it set overnight. This prevents the necklace from springing back to a straight shape. Remove the leather center and *voila!* you have made a necklace with that delicate filigree look. These necklaces can be oxided, too.

You can also make a wider filigree by preparing a 5-prong black leather center insertion, and crocheting your wire on the 5-prong wooden spool. As mentioned above, keep in mind that after you twist the necklace, it loses a bit of length, so compensate for this by making your necklace a bit longer. For example, if you wish a 16" necklace, crochet 18" of wire around the leather. At any rate, these necklaces are both delicate and beautiful.

Filigree Necklace
Oxidized Silver

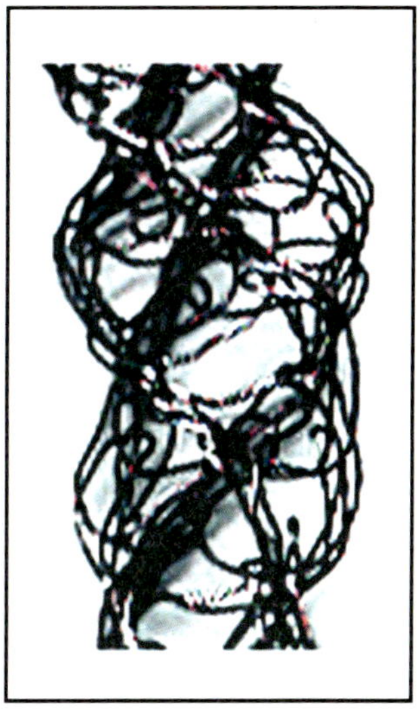

Another variation is to crochet the wire using the East-West/North-South or the Snake pattern with 4mm crystals or pearls or semi-precious stones, thereby adding yet another dimension to the filigree necklace.

18K Gold Necklace with Diamond Crystals

XXII. IT'S A WRAP!. . .PATTERN

This design was developed as an outgrowth of the weave-in-weave pattern. I wanted to create a necklace or bracelet that would highlight semi-precious stones more effectively. Rather than weaving one delicate crocheted necklace into another, usually three different weaves (one into the second and then into the third), which is very time consuming, I developed this new pattern, which I call, "It's a Wrap!"

Here is an example for a bracelet:

First part:

Using 24-gauge fine silver, double stitch, on a 4-prong wooden spool, crochet a length of 5", more for a larger wrist. Then, pull the crocheted bracelet through the wooden drawplate until it reaches 7". You do not want to pull the bracelet too tightly or you will not be able to finish the second half of the pattern.

Second part:

Cut a length of 14" of the 24-gauge fine silver. This is approximately twice the length of the 7" bracelet. Starting at one end, insert the fine silver through the bracelet, add a semi-precious bead, then make a quarter-turn and insert the silver again, add your bead, quarter-turn again, insert the silver, add your bead until you reach the other end. Secure the silver with your findings at each end.

It's a Wrap with Garnets

Making a **circular pattern** around the bracelet. **B** = Bead

________B_______B_______B_______B

The possibilities for this pattern are numerous. The nicest part of this design is that the beads literally protrude from the bracelet, but remain secure since each one is threaded individually and anchored through the bracelet.

XXIII. MESH NECKLACES

A new design which has a 21st Century look is the woven necklace with mesh enhancement. Using a 4-prong wooden spool, single stitch, 24-gauge fine silver wire, weave about 15" of wire. For a thinner necklace pull the necklace through a draw plate. If not, just leave it alone. Now you are ready to insert the woven necklace into a fine mesh. Use your wooden pick to open one end of the mesh and feed it on to your pick until it is finished.

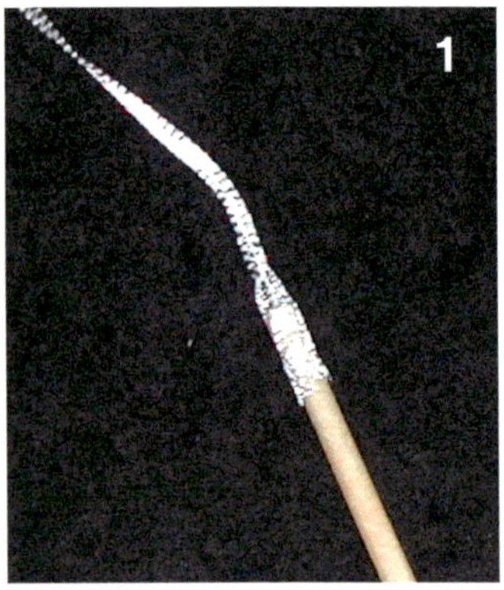

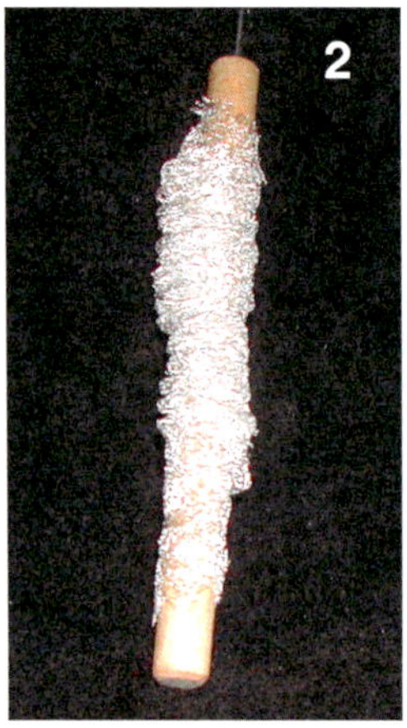

Next, feed the woven necklace into the mesh very gently. The mesh is fragile, but if you are careful, it will not break. Ending your work is very easy. I use 5mm crimping endcaps to hold the thick ends in place. Most jewelry supply sources stock this large endcap. *(See Metalliferous and M. Toback in Sources Section.)*

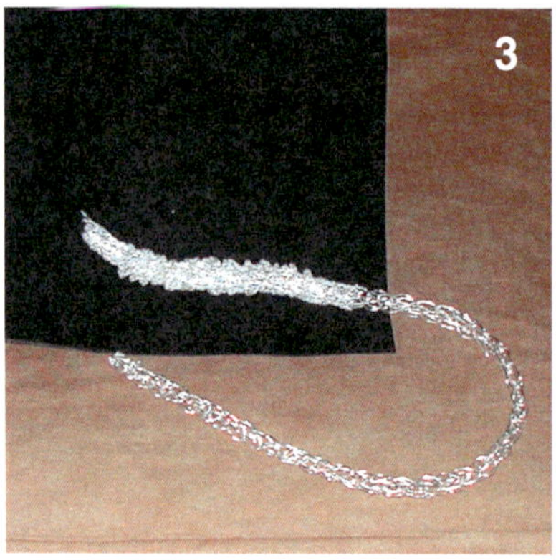

This is an example of the new design enhanced with a slide.

There are many variations for this mesh necklace. The mesh is 6mm wide and one meter long. This will be more than enough to produce a beautiful necklace. The 6mm mesh is available from Fire Mountain Gems, Rio Grande and Alacarte Clasps (the one company that manufactures this mesh in 20mm and 6mm). You can buy this mesh in many, many colors. Use silver, gold, pink, black, green or blue mesh over gold or silver. This is a diverse and easy way to make a necklace that is totally different. (See Supply Source section.)

XXIV. HOW TO END YOUR WORK / SECURING THE ENDS

CASTING OFF

When finishing a necklace, bracelet or earring, you have to cast off the wire loops from the wooden spool. It is a simple technique. For a single stitch just gently lift the loops over each cotter pin and remove from the spool. For a double stitch there are two loops remaining on each cotter pin. Lift each loop over the top once and you will have only one row of loops remaining. Lift the last row of loops over the cotter pins and remove from the spool. For a triple stitch you have three loops remaining. Follow the same method as described for a double stitch, reducing the loops until there are none remaining on your wooden spool.

WRAPPING

After adding the findings (endcaps, S-shaped closures, lobster claws, toggles, etc.), use 26-gauge fine silver and tightly wrap a coil around each end. Starting at the end of the finding, wrap the silver about half-inch, and insert the loose end into the weave. The end is actually hidden inside and does not come in contact with the wrist. If it did, it could scratch the skin. This is not very complicated and just takes practice. Additionally, make sure the silver coils are wrapped tightly to prevent them from unraveling.

Florette Bracelet with Wire Wrap to Secure the Ends

A necklace is easy to clasp and once secured, doesn't knock up against furniture such as tables, chairs and vanities. A bracelet takes much more abuse because it is often difficult to close with one hand. Therefore, a bracelet is often pulled, leaned on and twisted. OK – I made my point!

CRIMPING

Another means of securing the ends is to squeeze an endcap that can be crimped, before adding the findings. There are a large variety of endcaps that can be crimped. You can purchase them at Metalliferous or Myron Tobak (see Supply Source list). Make sure the endcap you purchase is not skimpy. It should be heavy gauge, preferably 14 to 22-gauge thick and not wiggle loosely after it is crimped. Remember that the end gap hole opening must be a minimum of 2.5 to 3.5mm.

COLD CONNECTIONS
And SOLDERING CONNECTION TECHNIQUES

It is important to learn both ways of completing your project. For those who do not want to use the Blazer GB2001 small butane torch, you will have to master the cold connection technique. It is a simpler way of ending your work and can be mastered in very little time. I always use a lead of crocheted rows to enable a quick and easy ending. Using your pick make a round end to insert into an endcap and then add a jump ring. It looks like this:

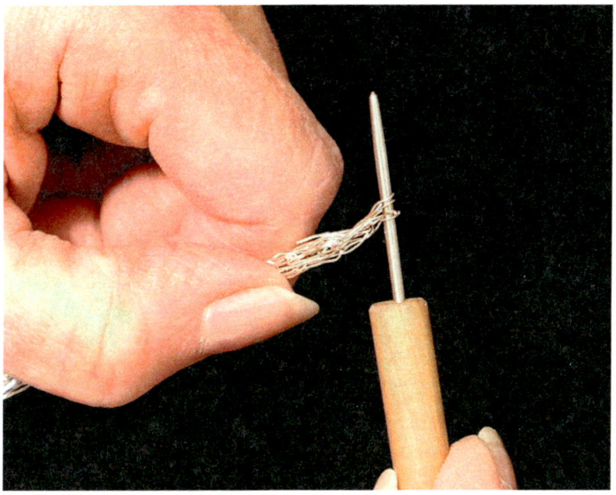

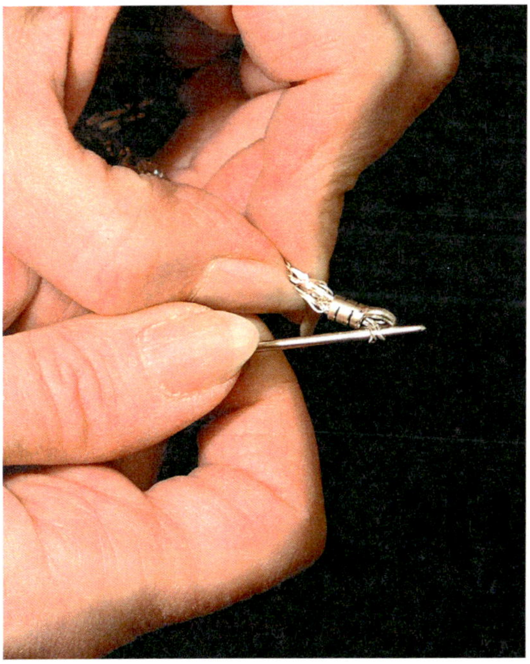

(Below) Add a jump ring with the finding of your choice.

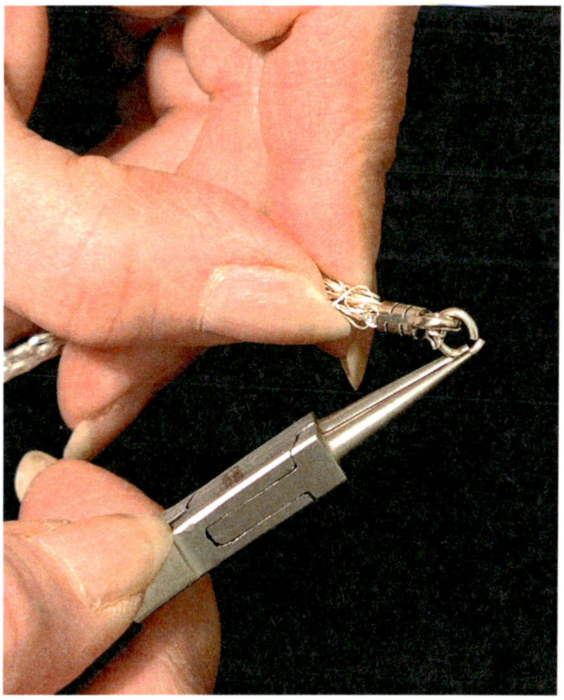

Then use a crimpable endcap, add a lobster claw, spring ring or toggle and you have a completed necklace or bracelet.

For a soldered end to your necklace or bracelet, use an endcap that is closed. Insert tiny pieces of solder (Stay-Brite) into your endcap and add the liquid flux, then insert the end of your lead into the endcap. Using your Blazer GB2001 lightly pass the flame over the endcap until you see a tiny puff of smoke. This will indicate the solder has flowed. It flows very quickly at 430° and will not burn your thin wire. You will notice that the ends turn a bit black. Do not worry about this since it can be easily cleaned using warm soapy water and *Instant Dip Silver Cleaner*. I prefer *Tide* liquid, but any liquid soap will work just fine. **1**. Dip your piece in the warm, soapy water. **2**. Next, dip your piece in the *Instant Dip Silver Cleaner.* **3.** Thoroughly rinse in clear water. **4.** Clean the ends with a brass brush for a brilliant shine.

XXV. SPECIALTY WOODEN SPOOLS

SMALL 8-PRONG AND 10-PRONG SPOOLS

Over the past six months, I have been negotiating with the company that manufactures wooden spools. In my quest for a spool that has eight prongs to create a finer weave, Good Wood Looms *(see Source List for address)* now manufactures an 8-prong spool and even a 10-prong spool. The possibilities with these new spools are fantastic. Below is an example of a finer woven bracelet.

Small 8-Prong Wooden Spool

Cherry Quartz Bracelet in Fine Silver

Using 30-gauge fine silver with a triple stitch, I made this bracelet and then inserted a 24-gauge wire strung with faceted cherry quartz. This is a simple woven bracelet, but with the insert of the cherry quartz, the bracelet has a very lacy look. Adding soldered endcaps and a safety chain the bracelet is beautiful.

Large 8-Prong Wooden Spool

LARGE 8-PRONG WOODEN SPOOL

I was determined to find a spool that can accommodate large crystals, semi-precious stones, chips and pearls. Standard wooden spools only have an inch opening and could not accomodate large crystals, semi-precious stones, chips and pearls. From my schematic drawing of an 8-prong wooden spool with a 2" opening, Good Wood Looms will now manufacture this larger wooden spool. An example of a turquoise necklace made with this new spool is stylish and worth all my efforts.

Turquoise Necklace in Fine Silver

Using a double stitch of 30-gauge fine silver, I inserted two small 2mm turquoise chips between every other cotter pin on the large 8-prong wooden spool.

Prepare a lead of four rows on cotter pins 1, 3, 5 and 7. Then between cotter pin one and three, add 2 chips; between cotter pin three and five, add 2 chips; between cotter pin five and seven, add 2 chips; between seven and one, add 2 chips; skip cotter pin eight and repeat starting with the first cotter pin. In between each row, I wove one row without any turquoise chips. This stunning necklace is very simple and easy to master.

CONCLUSION

The basic inspiration for my designs was discovering ways of using wooden spools to crochet and weave patterns incorporating pearls, fancy beads and crystals. Over time, I developed many creative patterns, some were by trial and error, some during a dream state and others using standard mathematical configurations.

I hope this book has given you a solid working knowledge of my techniques and patterns. There are many more designs that can be developed using these simple methods. For example, in my chapter on the weave-in-weave design, you may wish to insert a velvet ribbon, a rubber tube, curled mesh metal, large strands of pearls and many other fashionable inserts. You can also twist two necklaces together to achieve an entirely different look. Let your imagination aid you in creating designs that are both beautiful and fashionable. Good Luck!

Private instruction is available. Please contact Rita Scher by e-mail: Marga923@aol.com.

Her jewelry is available at:

Access Artisans

22 Greenwich Ave.
New York, NY 10011
212-337-9690

7 Grand Central Station MC67
New York, NY 10017
212-682-3049

SUPPLY SOURCES

The following is a list of suppliers for wooden spools, findings, sterling and fine silver, copper, gold, craft wire and tools. (* indicates where ***Jewelry Weaving for Everyone*** is available.)

A. HERSCHLAG, INC.
21 West 47th Street
New York, NY 10036
(212) 921-2660
(Good source for 18K findings)

ALACARTE CLASPS
P.O. Box 977
Forestville, CA 95436
(707) 887-2825
(Source for 6mm and 20mm mesh)

ALLCRAFT*
135 West 29th Street, Room 205
New York, NY 10001
(212) 279-7077
(Silver, gold, findings and tools)

BIG STONE BEADS AND FINDINGS
1180 Broadway
New York, NY 10001
(212) 779-9888
(Good source for Swarovski crystals, pendants, 14K gold, semi-precious stones and findings)

CK GEMS
12 West 37th Street 12th Floor
New York, NY 10018
(212) 683-0297
(Good source for pearls and beads)

CRYSTAL FINDINGS
1229-30 Chestnut Street, Suite 101
Philadelphia, PA 19107
(877) 955-3555
Good source for Swarovski crystals. Minimum order 1,000. Good prices, good selection, fast delivery)

FIRE MOUNTAIN GEMS*
One Fire Mountain Way
Grants Pass, OR 97526-2373
800-355-2137 (orders)
800-423-2319 (customer service)
Website: www.firemountaingems.com
(Great catalog for crystals, synthetic stones, semi-precious stones, findings and silver)

GOOD WOOD LOOMS*
P.O. Box 987
Langley, WA 98260
Tel & Fax: (360) 730-1826
Email: goodwood@whidbey.com
Website: www.goodwoodlooms.com
(Supplier for wooden spools)

HAUSER & MILLER CO.
10950 Lin-Valle Drive
St. Louis, MO 63123
800-462-7447
(Fine silver wire, 14K and 18K gold wire. Free catalog)

HOUSE OF INDIA
World Trade Center #7953
Dallas, TX 75258
800-527-7139
(A source for Swarovski crystals. Minimum order, 1,000)

K. GOTTFRIED, INC.
49 West 37th Street, 15th Floor
New York, NY 10018
212-391-4114 or 800-468-3743
(Great source for Swarovski crystals. Minimim order, 10 gross)

MARGOLA IMPORTS
48 West 37th Street
New York, NY 10008
212-695-1115
(Good source for Czech crystals, fire-polished glass and leather)

METALLIFEROUS*
34 West 46th Street
New York, NY 10036
(212) 944-0909
Fax (212) 944-0644
(The very best place to buy all supplies, except gold. They even stock the wooden spools and a line of crystals, beads and semi-precious stones)

MYRON TOBACK
25 West 47th Street
New York, NY 10036
(212) 779-9888
(Good source for silver, gold and findings)

PRECIOUS METALS WEST/FINE GOLD
608 S. Hill Street, Suite 407
Los Angeles, CA 90014
800-999-7528
Website: www.preciousmetalswest.com
(Source for 18K Extreme Easy solder)

RIO GRANDE
7500 Bluewater Road, NW
Albuquerque, NM 87121
800-545-6566
(Large selection of findings, silver, beads, gold-filled wire and just about everything to meet your needs. Free catalog)

RISHASHAY
300 Evans Avenue
Missoula, MT 59807
800-517-3311
(Great source for findings, silver beads and connectors. Free catalog)

SANTA FE JEWELRY SUPPLY
1513 Fifth Street
Santa Fe, NM 87505
800-659-3835
(Good source for tools, findings and beads)

TAJ
42 West 48th Street, Room 203
New York, NY 10036
(212) 944-6330
(Large selection of beads and semi-precious stones. Good source for pearls)

TSI, Inc.
101 Nickerson Street
P.O. Box 9266
Seattle, WA 98109
800-426-9984
(Great source for crystals, beads, tools and findings. Free catalog)

Turquoise Necklace in Fine Silver